9/93

CAUTION!

THIS MAY BE AN ADVERTISEMENT

A TEEN GUIDE TO ADVERTISING
BY KATHLYN GAY

FRANKLIN WATTS
New York ▪ London ▪ Toronto ▪ Sydney

Acknowledgments

I am grateful to those who shared information and offered advice while I was writing this book. Special thanks to George Taylor, Vice President, Creative and Production, Turtledove Clemens, Inc. and the Oregon Health Division; the Advertising Museum and visiting students from Columbia Academy, Portland, Oregon; Patrice Barnes, marketing research supervisor, Philadelphia, Pennsylvania; Peter Spencer, Executive Editor, Consumers' Research; *Charlotte Baecher, Editor,* Zillions; *Janet Hathaway, National Resources Defense Council; the U.S. Consumer Product Safety Commission and the U.S. Food and Drug Administration; Miles, Inc.; Doris Kimmel, who conducted research on effects of advertising; Douglas Gay, commercial artist, who shared his experiences in advertising agencies; the Charles Ammerman family; and my granddaughter, Nissa, and other family members, friends, and acquaintances who have described their responses to advertising messages.*

All photographs courtesy of the author except: Doris Kimmel: pp. 2, 3, 8; Oregon Health Division/Turtledove Clemens Inc./Jerry LaRocca: p. 9; Douglas Gay: p. 10; Martin Gay: p. 16 bottom.

Library of Congress Cataloging-in-Publication Data

Gay, Kathlyn.
    Caution! this may be an advertisement : a teen guide to advertising / by Kathlyn Gay.
        p.   cm.
    Includes bibliographical references and index.
    Summary: Examines the persuasive techniques used by advertisers and their effects on the consumer.
    ISBN 0-531-11039-7
    1. Advertising—Juvenile literature.   2. Advertising and children—Juvenile literature.   3. Youth as consumers—Juvenile literature.
    [1. Advertising.]   I. Title.
    HF5829.G30   1992
    659.1—dc20   91-38159   CIP   AC

CONTENTS

CHAPTER ONE

COME BUY

It's morning. You've turned on the radio or TV and almost miss the weather report because of a seemingly endless number of commercials.

You flip through the morning newspaper and the ads seem to crowd out the news.

Riding to school, you see many more types of ads: billboards, neon signs, cards in store windows, posters, replicas of products (such as the giant tire in front of the gas station), familiar symbols (such as the golden arches of McDonald's). Buses and taxis are plastered with advertising posters, and even many of the people you pass are wearing T-shirts, sweatshirts, jackets, or caps with the names of companies or products on them.

After school, you go to the supermarket. Most of the products you buy have some kind of advertising messages on them. So do the bags and boxes used to carry your purchases home.

In a school, in a government building, even in a church or temple, you will see advertisements, some of them requesting donations, others selling products, and still others advertising available jobs or services. Ads and commercials even pour into your home. In today's mail you might find a flyer from the local supermarket advertising the week's sales, a campaign brochure from a political candidate, a letter asking you to buy tickets to a concert, magazines with pages and pages of ads, and perhaps even a sample product. If the television or radio is on, you are inundated with more commercials.

THOUSANDS AND THOUSANDS OF ADS

All day long, advertisements come your way—from a message on a matchbox or even a doormat to a gigantic sign on a blimp or a banner trailing behind a plane high above you. An hour-long radio broadcast can include up to forty commercials, and the typical American sees over 250,000 television commercials by the time he or she leaves high school. (Some researchers say the number of TV commercials viewed can be as high as 50,000 per year.) And if you read through an entire Sunday edition of *The New York Times*, you could be subjected to up to 350 pages of ads.[1]

On average, Americans are "bombarded by 5,000 advertising messages per day, and the number of ads is expected to increase steadily," according to international marketing consultants Stan Rapp and Tom Collins. Of course, no one actually is aware of being exposed to that many advertising messages. As the marketing consultants pointed out, people remember only 2 to 3 percent of the commercial messages they are exposed to daily.[2]

Even then, it is uncertain just how much consumers absorb from the ads they see and hear and how those ads affect them. People have argued for decades about the effects of TV commercials on young people, for example. Some surveys show that teenagers seldom pay attention to commercials, while others indicate that sales tend to increase when products geared for teenagers are advertised on television.

Some argue that advertising persuades consumers (all who use goods and services) to act against their own best interests. Perhaps that is true in some cases. But then again the power of advertising to persuade may be overstated at times.

Here's how Nissabeth of southern California, who calls herself "an almost typical teenager," perceives the role of advertising:

"I think many kids buy things because of advertising and because they think it is the cool thing to do—especially when their favorite celebrity is advertising or endorsing a product. Like, many kids buy Coke because of who's advertising it. But I don't believe in buying something because your friends do or because you feel pressured by advertising. I think people should like what they're buying and buy because of their tastes, not because of their friends' tastes."

In a critical look at TV commercials in particular, Nissabeth observed: "The teenagers and others shown on TV commercials are *so* fake! Okay, maybe the thing they are advertising is fun or nice or whatever, but they exaggerate *so* much. It doesn't seem realistic to me. They [the actors and actresses] make everything look so wonderful. If gullible kids and their parents believe them, they will run right out and buy, buy, buy!"[3]

WHAT IS ADVERTISING?

Just as opinions vary on the power of advertising, so there are diverse views on how advertising should be defined. The term advertising frequently refers to an industry—that is, the people who design and create advertising for print and broadcast commercials.

"Mass persuasion" is one way people who prepare advertising explain what they do. Others define the act of advertising as keeping a company's name in the public eye, or "teaching" people to want things, or informing the public about goods and services and how they can benefit consumers.

Advertising also has been called a propelling power, as important as the energy required to move the machinery of industry. Some economists have described advertising (in all its forms) as an activity that furnishes valuable information to consumers and that is vital to a free market economy. The free flow of advertising information, these economists say, keeps prices lower and quality higher than would be possible if advertising were restricted.

For this book, advertising is defined as a way to inform, to sell, and to promote. It is an activity that we all engage in at some time or another—during job interviews (we advertise our skills and personality), while conducting garage sales, when campaigning for politicians or causes, and on many other occasions. In fact, some type of advertising or persuasion was used to convince someone to buy this book you are reading.

U.S. advertisers spend hundreds of *billions* of dollars each year pursuing their selling goals. Although advertising does not have the power to compel you to buy, it does "have the power to *prevail*," as one professor of advertising put it.[4]

In other words, over time, advertising in a variety of media can have a collective effect. Hearing or seeing a message over and over again may influence not only what we buy but also how we vote, or help determine the causes we support.[5]

One of the purposes of this book is to show the kinds of persuasive techniques advertisers use and how advertising messages are conveyed through diverse kinds of media and/or promotional materials. Some of the ongoing debates about the effects of advertising on consumers also are covered. In addition, the book includes some guidelines on how you can determine whether you are buying on the basis of factual information about goods and services or because of advertising techniques and methods designed to influence your choices.

Some advertising methods have been used for centuries; others are based on technology developed only a few decades ago. Nevertheless, old or new, the goals of advertisers are the same: they want you to choose (buy) their goods or services over those of the competition.

CHAPTER TWO

FROM STREET CRIERS TO PEDDLERS

"Whatdyalack? Whatdyalack-whatdyalack-whatdya-lack?" The rhythmic cry was a common one in the streets of England for many centuries, perhaps beginning about the 1300s. The hawker, or crier, walked the streets, shouting the question in doorways of homes, or asking passersby: "What do you lack (what do you need)?," running the words together in a loud chant.

The crier would likely break the chant with "Come buy! Come buy my roses and lavender!" Or "Come buy my rabbits! Come buy of me!" Another hawker would chant or sing the praises of oysters for sale, another would call attention to fine herring, and still others wanted to sell umbrellas or mousetraps. Or a chimney sweep would call: "I sweep your chimney clean, O!" Other tradespeople offered to mend pots and kettles, or old chairs. "Knives to sharpen?" was a common call.

A baker would chant "Buy my crumpets, O! Muffins today. Hot, hot, hot!" A pastry maker had "Hote pyes, hote" (hot pies) for sale. Or a crier would call in a sing-song verse that rang through the town:

Hot cross buns!
Hot cross buns!
One-a-penny!
Two-a-penny!
Hot cross buns!

Many street cries such as this one were written down and in later years were recited by children. Such nursery rhymes are still repeated today, but few realize that they were originally a form of advertising. In fact, town criers and hawkers ringing bells and chanting and shouting in the streets were some of the first advertisers. Their shouts and chants called attention to the goods and services they were offering for sale.

Street calls and cries are among the earliest forms of advertising. They were heard thousands of years ago in Greece, for example, as hawkers announced goods for sale ranging from cattle to cosmetics. But vocal appeals were not the only form of early advertising. Ancient people— Sumerians, Egyptians, Greeks, and Romans among them—also used a written medium, carving hieroglyphics, or picture symbols, into stone walls and monuments, and writing on papyrus, a form of paper made from papyrus reeds. But the ads did not always try to persuade people to buy goods or services. Rather, they commonly offered rewards for runaway slaves or servants or for lost household items or personal belongings.

However, only a few people in ancient societies could decipher the written language. Thus, merchants not only used street criers to advertise their wares, but also put up various tools or signs that identified their trade. A crude picture of a grain mill carved into stone or wood identified a bakery. A picture of a goat indicated a dairy, and a green bush hung above a doorway was a common symbol for a winemaker.

What if you'd been a stranger in town and wanted to

find the local school? You'd look for a sign showing a boy being whipped. The sign not only represented the kind of discipline used to force young boys to obey, but also the fact that girls were not allowed in formal schools.

WRITINGS ON A WALL

In ancient Rome, people also scratched ads on stone walls and buildings. But simply etching symbols into stone was rather dull. Advertisers soon discovered that color helped attract attention.

For example, if you lived in a Roman city during that time and wanted to rent your house, you would place your ad on the outer wall of your home. First you would white-wash a section, perhaps near the door, and then paint in black or vivid red "House for Rent."[1]

Painted ads, however, appeared more often in public places. City or courtyard walls or the exteriors of public buildings were like the graffiti-filled walls in today's urban centers. Pictures and symbols were painted wherever there was an empty space. If a wall filled up with ads, a spot would be whitewashed and a new message painted on, urging people to come to such events as plays, circuses, or fresh-water baths.

Though wall signs were popular, they almost disappeared after the Roman Empire collapsed. Conquerors who dominated Rome for many centuries did not value learning and literacy. Thus, for nearly one thousand years few advances were made in any form of communication.

The need for advertising also declined. Since there was little respect for private property, shops frequently were ransacked and goods were stolen. Merchants were afraid to let anyone except trusted friends know what stocks they had.

But by the 1300's, merchants had started to organize, creating protective leagues to guard their property. Trade and business improved. Along with economic advances came better education and living standards, which in turn brought the need for advertising to sell an increasing number of goods and services. The songs and chants of criers again filled the streets. In major European cities, tavern owners frequently hired criers to advertise the wines and ales served. Sometimes the criers blew horns to draw a crowd, offering samples of wine and giving directions on how to reach the tavern.

ADS IN PRINT

Some of the first written ads in England were hand-lettered public announcements. Professional scribes prepared these notices, called *siquis*, a term that came from the Latin words *si quis*, meaning "if anybody." Ancient Romans used that phrase on public notices that often began, "If anybody knows of . . ." (the whereabouts of a lost article) or "If anybody desires. . ." (to buy a certain product, such as perfume or coffee).

The first siquis in England were posted by clergymen, teachers, and other professionals seeking positions. Later, after movable type was developed in the 1400s, one of the first published ads was a siquis that was posted on churches throughout London. The siquis announced the sale of books used in religious services. William Caxton, author of the ad as well as the books, noted that buyers could "have them good chepe [cheap]."

Over the years, many printed flyers and posters advertising goods and services were tacked up on buildings, a practice still followed today in many countries. Yet the vast majority of people in England and other parts of Europe still were not able to read, so vocal advertising did not disappear. Picture signs or trade symbols on buildings also were in demand. Following a well-established practice by then, shopkeepers, merchants, and tavern owners in Britain used bells, bulls, dolphins, crosses, globes, dragons, lions, stars, and many other kinds of symbols over doorways to help customers identify places of business and to advertise them. Frequently, people agreed to "meet at the sign of the mermaid," for example, or perhaps "under the sign of the lion."

One type of early trade sign that still prevails in a few places today is the barber pole painted with red and white stripes. However, the stripes signified blood-letting, which was the barber's original line of work. It was common practice to cut and bleed people as a "cure" for a variety of diseases. A blood-letter could increase his income by cutting hair as a trade.

As literacy spread across Europe in the 1600s, publishers began to print newspapers, or more correctly newsbooks—booklets or pamphlets that contained news. Yet the news was not current as we know it today. Newsbooks might be published once a year or every two or three years. They contained ads called "advices," a term that stemmed from the Offices of Publick Advice in London, where a weekly news sheet was published. Some of the most common advices were designed to sell land, books, or some type of health "cure."

As England and other European nations established colonies abroad, printed advertising became increasingly important. Ads described the products available from the colonies and the benefits of selling manufactured goods to settlers in foreign lands.

Colonists also made use of printed ads. In colonial America, for example, an ad in the first issue of the *Boston News Letter*, published on April 24, 1704, carried a notice requesting advertisements from people who had merchandise to sell or property to rent or sell. Readers also were urged to place ads asking for the return of lost or stolen items. Thereafter, weekly issues of the newspaper carried simple ads sold at what the publisher described as reasonable rates.

But newspapers did not become a widely used medium for ads until Benjamin Franklin began publishing the

Pennsylvania Gazette in 1729. Because of Franklin's style of writing and liberal use of ads in his Philadelphia newspaper, people began to realize that newspaper ads could help sell goods and services.

Following Franklin's lead, other newspapers in major cities increased their advertising, which helped speed up sales of the publications as well. Another factor was also responsible for more newspapers being sold. Ads were as much news as they were appeals to buy. Some ads, for example, announced the arrival of ships carrying cargo from Europe—a major event in the lives of colonists. People gathered at docks and in warehouses to look over goods being introduced for the first time in the new land.

In later years, another type of newspaper ad became popular: the personal notice. Usually, the ads announced that a couple had separated or divorced and one spouse would not be responsible for the other's debts. Many of the ads were in verse and concluded with such lines as:

I will not pay one single fraction
For any debt of _____'s contraction.

Newspaper advertising continued to increase along with the number of newspapers published in the United States. But few people outside the larger cities had access to newspapers. In the first place, only a few paper mills were operating, and paper for printing was not readily available. As a result, only a small number of newspapers were printed each day. Another drawback to mass distribution was the lack of a system to transport and deliver large numbers of daily papers beyond the city limits.[2]

PEDDLERS—ADVERTISERS ON-THE-GO

Because people in remote areas of the United States seldom saw printed ads, rural folks had to learn about products from peddlers. Most peddlers were men who began their trade while in their late teens or early twenties. Before the 1800s, a peddler usually traveled on foot, carrying goods in double packs, one strapped to his back and the other across his chest. Because the packs weighed a total of about 100 pounds, a peddler needed a walking stick to help him trudge along muddy, rutted roads, up hills, and through woods and swamps as he went from one rural house to another.

And what was inside his packs? He carried practical items like socks, work pants, needles, and thread, and yard goods such as lace or cotton cloth. Clocks, jewelry, and spices were part of the pack, too.

Many of the first peddlers in the United States also carried goods they had manufactured themselves— household utensils, for example. If these home-manu-factured items did not sell, the peddler might trade them for clothing, blankets, or other necessities that his neigh-bors produced and then market or sell these to people in nearby settlements.

Although many rural folks looked forward to a peddler's visit, the peddler had to find ways to persuade people to buy, using some selling techniques still common today. Perhaps he made farmers feel good about themselves by praising the fitness of their children or the healthy crops they were growing in the fields. A peddler might convince people that they should buy because their neighbors had found his shovels sturdy or his spices just right for making soups. Or he might give away some special treat—nutmeg from the West Indies was a popular item—to convince peo-ple that they ought to buy more of his products because they were "special."

Some peddlers could afford a horse or mule, which was loaded with goods and led along a trail, easing the burden that the salesman-advertiser had to bear. As roads im-proved, more and more peddlers traveled by wagon, haul-ing an even wider variety of articles for sale.

A peddler's wagon was in itself a form of advertising. It was painted in bright colors—reds and yellows with complementary blues and greens. Everybody in town knew when a peddler had arrived. Pots and pans, picks and shovels clanged against the sides of the wagon. Bells on horses jangled. The peddler might play a guitar or harmonica.

Many a wagon peddler carried medicinal herbs and other preparations that were supposed to cure ailments. The medicine man, as he was called, described his remedies in glowing terms and offered samples. Very few of these "cure-alls" had any healing effect, but the peddler put on a good show, and people bought the products.[3]

URBAN PEDDLERS

In the larger American cities of the late 1800s and early 1900s, the peddler was also a familiar figure. Although his advertising and selling were similar to the pack peddlers in the rural areas, the city peddler usually pushed a cart loaded with yard goods, vegetables, fish, or cooking utensils. Sometimes he specialized in such items as pants and suspenders. He walked the city streets, calling out the items for sale like the street criers of times past.

Until a few decades ago, peddlers were a part of street life in cities and towns across the United States. Like Europeans of earlier times, they offered to sharpen knives, mend furniture and umbrellas, or to sell you "Fresh fish!" or "Bananas! Buy a bunch!" or "Fresh flowers!" They created a supermarket of the streets. None of the products were packaged in colorful and convenient boxes, cans, or other containers, because the peddlers needed none of these to attract customers. Their cries and chants, or the clang of bells on their carts brought the buyers out.

With the advent of railroads and train travel, another type of peddler, called a drummer, appeared. The drummer was so-named because of his large trunk, known as a drum, which was filled with Bibles, watches, clocks, combs, pencils, cloth, socks, and any number of other items that were offered for sale.

During the 1900s, further development of transportation systems helped put many peddlers out of business. Trucks traveling on cross-country highways, planes, and trains carried goods to stores in most parts of the nation. As a result, many former peddlers became permanent residents of communities and opened hardware, grocery, and variety stores.

Door-to-door salespeople followed in the footsteps of the peddlers of the past, offering goods like brushes and spices and magazines for sale. Although some door-to-door selling still goes on, that kind of marketing no longer fits into the life-style of most U.S. consumers.

In most families of the past, the father was the "breadwinner" working outside the home and the mother was the homemaker. The majority of households today do not fit this pattern. Well over half of all women are in the labor force. In single-parent households and in households where there are two or more wage-earners, seldom is a resident at home to respond to a salesperson who comes to the door.[4]

Today, department stores and supermarkets have taken the place of one-to-one selling and buying practices. And each year about 10,000 new products are offered to potential buyers in varied marketplaces.[5]

What will be sold? What kinds of marketplaces will be selected to sell a particular product or service? Who will be expected to buy? These are just some of the questions advertisers try to answer with the help of market researchers and consultants.

CHAPTER THREE

TO MARKET, TO MARKET. . . .

> To market, to market
> To buy a fat pig
> Home again, home again
> Jiggety-jig

These lines from an old nursery rhyme describe a type of market that has been in existence since ancient times—a central place such as a village square or a crossroads where people can go to buy food, clothing, and other necessities. Open-air markets where vendors sell goods ranging from bananas to wheelbarrows are still active in most parts of the world. In the United States, they include farmers' markets, fish markets, and huge flea markets where hundreds of vendors offer a cornucopia of goods. In urban areas today, a marketplace also can be a corner grocery or pharmacy, a neighborhood shopping center, a business section in a town or city, or a supermarket.

A marketplace might also be a row of vending machines or a garage sale or a home sales party where invited guests try out and buy cosmetics, jewelry, toys, or other products. Or it could be a TV channel—home shoppers tune in to shopping channels where sellers advertise products ranging from clothing to tools.

However, those who produce and sell goods and services—usually referred to as advertisers—think of a market in other terms as well. Frequently, advertisers define a market as a particular geographic region, such as the southwestern or northeastern part of the United States. Or the marketplace might be the entire nation or another country, such as Germany or Japan. It could also be a category of people such as teenagers, the elderly, doctors, or an ethnic group (those who share a way of life) who may or may not be in one specific location. Markets, then, are groups of people who share certain characteristics and are potential buyers for particular products.

Before trying to sell their goods or services, many advertisers want to know which group would be most likely to buy. Knowledge about a group of consumers helps companies to position what they have to sell. In other words, they try to present a product or service in such a way that it will appeal to a specific group.

BEHIND THE SCENES

How is information about consumer groups compiled? Some advertisers and people who work as advertising professionals gather their own data, using library reference materials and conducting informal surveys to solicit opinions about products from friends and acquaintances. In some cases, advertising professionals depend on their own experiences or personal feelings about products to create ads or promotional campaigns, or they may use promotional techniques that have worked for others.

Increasingly, however, advertisers are turning to market researchers who compile data about consumer groups. Rather than make subjective judgments (based on personal views) about what consumers need and want, market researchers collect factual information—statistics on people's buying habits, tests of consumer reactions to products, and studies of what motivates consumers to buy certain things.

After analyzing the data, the experts draw their conclusions about market groups. Seldom do products that cost millions of dollars to develop go to market without such research. Why? Because out of the thousands of new products and services offered to consumers each year, about one in three fail, in spite of extensive advertising efforts.[1]

Even in your neighborhood supermarket, hundreds of new items probably are introduced each year. In one supermarket in the Northwest, for example, more than 1,500 new products appear in the store annually, often with displays and sampling tests. But less than 10 percent of those products survive.[2]

In short, competition is fierce for many kinds of products. As consumers we can choose from among dozens of different types and brands of one kind of product— toothpaste, shampoo, deodorants, athletic shoes, jeans, fast-food restaurants, or blank tapes for music or videos are just a few examples.

One toothpaste may be very similar to another. All athletic shoes are constructed in similar ways. So why does one brand appeal more than another? That is what marketing experts try to find out. They analyze the behavior of consumers to try to learn how to appeal to them.

RESEARCH METHODS

Questionnaires and product-sample testing are research methods that many major U.S. companies have used for years to introduce new products. Company researchers may gather information about the kinds of toothpaste people prefer, for instance. Market surveys have shown that most consumers buy toothpaste not just because they need it but also because they want to look nice and "feel fresh." On the basis of such information, a company would develop a toothpaste that could be used like a cosmetic to brighten teeth, and also provide a fresh taste.

Samples of the product would then be mailed to households in such cities as Kansas City, Missouri; Spokane, Washington; Denver, Colorado; and Fort Wayne, Indiana. Researchers would select populations representing a cross-section of occupations, incomes, and life-styles. Thus, if testers liked the taste and texture of the product, other Americans would probably like it and buy it, too.

The field interview is another important research tool. An interviewer might go to a mall or supermarket to ask shoppers their opinions about specific products. Perhaps shoppers will taste-test samples of pizza or other food or a beverage product.

Maybe a new toy needs to be tested. "A shopper (usually a mother) with a small child might agree to take part in a test conducted in a private office or meeting room," says Patrice Barnes, who supervises a variety of market research studies for a management consultant firm in Philadelphia, Pennsylvania. She explained that "while the child plays with the toy, the researcher observes and records how the child reacts to and interacts with the toy, the length of time the youngster plays with it, and perhaps asks the mother's opinions about the toy."

Barnes also has set up many focus groups, each usually made up of ten people, bringing them together to learn how they feel about certain products. Although the consultant firm has conducted a broad range of research, from studies of roofing products to buying lottery tickets, "the majority—70 to 80 percent—of the research we do is in the medical field," Barnes says. "In such cases, our focus groups are made up of doctors, pharmacists, medical technicians, and other health-care personnel. They meet in a conference room and essentially examine and discuss the pros and cons of new prescription-type drugs or other medical products. The client—the manufacturer or someone representing the advertiser—sits in another room, listening and observing through a one-way window. By setting up and leading focus groups, we help advertisers determine how they should position and promote their products," she says.[3]

Focus groups also play a part in another research method. Potential consumers "test" print ads and TV commercials. That is, small groups of people look at ads and then answer questions about what they have seen, providing researchers with information about the impressions the ads have made.

In some cases, researchers try to find out how viewers react emotionally to ads, so that ads can "help establish an emotional bond between the consumer and the brand," as an executive with BBDO Worldwide advertising agency explained to marketing columnist Bruce Horovitz. To determine an emotional reaction, BBDO researchers ask viewers to look at a set of fifty-three photographs (called a photodeck) of actors who are smiling, frowning, pouting, or in some way depicting an emotion. Viewers select from the deck the photos that represent how they feel about an ad. Such research has helped determine the kind of images used in a number of major advertising campaigns, including General Electric's "We bring good things to life" commercials on TV. Some researchers say that use of such nonverbal means to measure advertising will increase in the years ahead.[4]

Within the past few years, some companies have developed market research programs, using their own data bases. Information on people who actually buy a company's products is compiled from printed questionnaires, warranty forms with customer survey questions, telephone and personal interviews, and identification codes on cents-off coupons.

If you redeem your cents-off coupon at a store, it will be returned with hundreds of others to marketing companies, to advertisers, or to manufacturers. Codes on the coupons tell research analysts where people bought the new product—in which kinds of stores and in what parts of the nation. In general, the codes help researchers draw conclusions about how well new products will be accepted.

Kraft General Foods (KGF), for example, recently mailed out discount coupons for its so-called light food products—those that are sugar-free and low in fat. The coupons have identification numbers that when redeemed show which type of household purchased KGF products. The data then are entered into a computer, creating consumer profiles, or biographical sketches.

Whether data is compiled from coupons or other sources, consumer profiles include much more information than what people buy. They also show ages, genders, educational levels, occupations, total annual income, hobbies, and sometimes even the politics and religion of those living in particular households. From these profiles, marketing experts can determine what kinds of products will appeal to a targeted group and can suggest the types of ads that will be most effective in promoting the company's products.

According to British journalist Eric Clark, who has investigated advertising in Europe and the United States, millions of American and European consumers

are constantly watched, quizzed, divided and examined in almost every conceivable group and subgroup. Their circumstances, beliefs, habits and behaviour are continuously measured and pored over. Trends are continually charted and analysed to help determine which products are likely to become ripe for selling.[5]

Yet the increasing number of marketing surveys could create a backlash among consumers. Some researchers report a significant decline in the number of people willing to take part in surveys that they recognize as marketing or advertising devices.

Nevertheless, the data gathering goes on, because researchers are attempting to learn how to design advertising to fit the needs of specific groups. According to marketing consultants Stan Rapp and Tom Collins, who advise businesses worldwide on marketing strategies, consumer data bases help advertisers relate to consumers in more personalized ways. Feedback from consumers can then help advertisers present sales messages to specific groups through a variety of techniques and media.[6]

GETTING THE MESSAGE INTO THE MEDIA

One advertising medium, of course, is word-of-mouth promotion—one person telling another about goods and services. That kind of advertising is still effective, especially for local businesses. However, when large corporations or nonprofit organizations plan advertising campaigns to reach groups of people nationwide, they usually depend on the creative staffs of their advertising departments or use independent advertising agencies.

Many major advertising agencies are concentrated along New York City's Madison Avenue, which is close to the headquarters of many national and international corporations. As a result, the term "Madison Avenue" has become a synonym for the word advertising (as in "Madison-Avenue techniques"). But successful advertising agencies also are located in other cities and towns across the United States as well as in other industrialized nations.

The creative staff in an advertising agency or department includes commercial artists, copywriters, creative directors, and others who develop ads. Usually, it is the job of these professionals to determine which media will be used to promote a particular product or service.

Frequently, when people talk or write about "the media," they mean television, radio, newspapers, and nationally distributed magazines. Indeed, these media make up a major part of the communication network in the United States and in many other nations as well. They provide information about local, state, and national events.

Some media are supported partially by subscribers, but most broadcast and print media actively solicit advertising from businesses wanting to reach a particular group of viewers, listeners, or readers. Many of the media depend on advertisements to stay in business, although that dependence varies with each medium. And the audiences, in turn, depend on the media for information about goods and services available.

Not surprisingly the top advertisers in the United States are well-known companies such as Procter & Gamble, Phillip Morris (which owns Kraft General Foods along with its tobacco companies), General Motors, PepsiCo, McDonald's, and Walt Disney. The nation's advertisers spent more than $41 billion to advertise on TV, radio, newspapers, magazines, and billboards) in 1990, the most recent year for which figures are available (reported by the industry magazine *Advertising Age*).[7]

More than double that amount was spent on other types of advertising media. Some are familiar, such as the advertising that comes directly to you through the mail or the solicitations that you receive by telephone. Other media include car cards that appear on buses, taxis, subway trains, trucks, and other commercial vehicles.

Sometimes vehicles are designed to be advertisements in themselves; they are shaped like a doughnut or hot dog or other product or they carry giant-sized objects—such as six-foot liquor bottles—on top of trucks, to attract attention. Another type of mobile advertisement features banners that are towed by airplanes, or ads printed on blimps and hot-air balloons.

Specialty items are still another kind of media for promotion. Most people have dozens of them around their homes. They include matchbooks, placemats, coffee mugs, pens, stickers, notebooks, calendars, and countless bric-a-brac that carry advertising and may be given away to promote products and services.

AN AD CAMPAIGN

With the many means of advertising and promotion available, ad practitioners must decide which to use to sell a product or service. This usually means developing a basic plan for an ad campaign. Some campaigns are designed to use the mass media, such as network television stations and nationally distributed magazines, to reach potential customers.

One example of a mass-marketing effort is the campaign developed for Flintstones Vitamins. Over two decades ago, Miles, Inc., one of the leading manufacturers of medicinals and vitamin supplements, decided to introduce a new chewable vitamin that would appeal to young children. At the time, only a few brands of chewable vitamins were being manufactured, and only one of the brands was in a shape other than the common "pillow" or pill form. Miles consulted not only with its product research scientists but also with its advertising agency in New York City. Together they decided to develop a new chewable vitamin that would appeal to children by its shape and would compete with the animal-shaped Pals brand already on the market.

How did the company decide what would be an appealing shape? They did so by using market research, which included asking hundreds of children to look at picture cards of different shapes—from cartoon characters to circus animals—and state their preferences. One of the picture cards showed the characters from "The Flintstones," which at the time was one of the most popular children's TV shows. In fact, Fred Flintstone's expression "Yabba dabba doo!" had become a part of kid lingo.

Since the Flintstone characters proved to be overwhelmingly popular with the research group as well, the next step was obtaining permission from Hanna-Barbera, creators of the animated cartoon show, to use the characters as shapes for a vitamin product. Miles paid a royalty fee for the use of Fred, Barney, Pebbles, Bamm-Bamm, Dino, and the Flintmobile and began production on its new product.

At the same time, the company's advertising agency was developing an ad campaign. The agency set up its objective, which was "to clearly communicate that the popular characters from the Flintstones show were appearing in six different shapes of vitamins, that the vitamins tasted good and were pleasant to take, and that one Flintstones tablet a day would provide the vitamins kids need if they don't eat properly," an agency spokesperson said.[8]

Because the Flintstones were already associated with TV, television was a logical medium for a major portion of the advertising. Commercials included episodes from the Flintstones program and were shown during weekend programs geared for children. The product also was introduced in magazines such as *Parents* and *Good Housekeeping* commonly read by mothers, who were the most likely buyers. In addition, ads were placed in medical journals to introduce the product to doctors who, in turn, might suggest the vitamin supplement for their young patients. Since sales of the Flintstones far surpassed other vitamins produced by the company at that time, the company concluded that the advertising campaign was a success.

Today many major marketing campaigns include not only the use of several media but also dialogue with consumers about the products they have purchased. Consumers "want to be vocal partners in the process of providing satisfactory goods and services," Rapp and Collins explained, describing how the process has worked for Gerber Products, which produces a variety of foods and other items for babies:

Every ad and piece of literature put out by Gerber encourages parents to call Gerber's 800 number for more information about the care and feeding of the baby. Gerber's receives some 1,200 calls a day. . . . The service offers a striking example of the value of the feedback obtained through dialogue with the consumer. So many callers asked about the edibility of half-eaten jars of baby food that the company decided to bring out smaller jars, so infants could finish a jar in a single feeding.[9]

PACKAGING

Along with market research and more personalized advertising campaigns, advertisers consider another factor when developing a product for a group of consumers. That is the packaging.

In the past, packaging primarily meant getting a product into a simple container—a jar, bottle, box, bag, tin, or crate—so that the item could be transported to a store and placed on a shelf until a customer bought it. Many products, however, were not individually packaged. In most grocery stores of the 1800s and early 1900s, people bought from bulk supplies—large barrels or bins filled with such foods as dried beans, rice, coffee, sugar, molasses, pickles, crackers, cookies, and dried fruits. A round or wheel of cheese would sit on a counter along with perhaps a large jug of vinegar or cider or a tin of syrup. If a customer bought a hunk of cheese, the grocer might wrap it in waxed paper or newspaper. Paper sacks were provided for some foods, but it was common for customers to bring their own containers to carry home the supplies they bought.

After World War II, the economy expanded greatly as manufacturers turned from making weapons and other goods for the armed forces to producing more and more consumer goods. As an increasing number of companies produced the same types of products, consumers could choose among a variety of breakfast cereals or soaps or household gadgets or other goods.

But how could advertisers convince consumers to choose the products that they manufactured or processed? One way was to offer convenience along with the products. That meant prepackaging many goods such as foods and beverages, hardware and automotive supplies, and cleaning compounds. Stores and shops could offer products not from bulk supplies but packaged and ready for a customer to buy.

Today, consumers are attracted to products that are not only prepackaged but packaged in easy-to-handle containers. Many beverages, vegetable oils, syrups, and other liquids are packaged in unbreakable plastic containers that consumers prefer over glass bottles that can break easily. Foods such as mustard and catsup are packaged in squeezable plastic bottles, making them easy to apply. Some products are packaged for easy carrying, such as packs of beverage cans held together with plastic rings or encased in a plastic wrap.

Many prepared foods such as puddings and foods for microwave cooking are packaged in single-serving containers, offering a convenience for those who do not prepare large amounts of food or who carry lunches. The single-serving beverage box has become one of the most popular convenience containers. Usually several of the beverage boxes are held together with a plastic wrap, another way to facilitate handling. More than four billion of these containers are sold each year.

In fact, the growing volume of packaging materials, including paper, glass, and aluminum, has been widely criticized. Many consumers are concerned about the packaging materials that end up in landfills, the places where municipal garbage is dumped. Since these landfills are packed tightly, materials do not decompose, or break down, quickly. Thus the sites fill up and have to close. New landfills are expensive to construct because they must be built to prevent toxins from seeping into groundwater below the earth's surface. Cities are trying to find alternative ways to deal with trash disposal, such as setting up recycling programs or increasing charges for garbage collection in order to encourage citizens to reduce the amount of trash they generate.

Some companies also are beginning to reduce the amount of material they use in packaging. A few put their products in containers that can be reused. Some glass jelly jars, for example, can be reused as drinking glasses, and some foods are packaged in cans or plastic bowls or tubs that can be reused for storage.

A reusable container might help sell a product, but very little of the total packaging for products sold in supermarkets, discount stores, and other retail stores is designed for that purpose. Most packaging is designed to provide a sales pitch—to attract attention and to motivate a consumer to buy.

Packaging plays a major role in sales pitches aimed at children. "Even more than advertising, packaging pervades the kid's world," according to James McNeal, a marketing professor at Texas A&M University. He points out that packages for such products as cereals, soft drinks, snacks, and even milk and ice cream give "visual sales talks." These packages serve as silent salespeople at home, in the store, and at school.[10]

For years, the makers of Cracker Jack have packaged their product in a box that advertised small novelties as prizes. The prizes help sell the product. Breakfast cereals also have a fairly long history of packaging designed to appeal to children. Along with colorful cartoon characters, cereal boxes picture "free" prizes or premiums inside. The "free" premium might be bubble gum, stickers, a toy, or a coupon for a "free" ice cream cone.

In a similar vein, several food processing companies now package single-serving frozen meals or pizzas in boxes clearly designed to get kids to buy or to urge adults to buy for them. The foods can be cooked in microwave ovens and are not much different from similar frozen food items packaged for adults, but the packages for kids feature drawings of cartoon characters who appear to be touting the foods pictured on the boxes. If the superstars of cartoon world are not enough to promote a sale, then perhaps the offer on a box for a "free funpak" or "free sticker set" inside will do the trick.

Companies also are packaging toiletries and cosmetics for young children—deodorants, shampoos, styling gels, lotions, and perfumes. Although children can and do use adult toiletries and cosmetics, those designed especially for kids between the ages of seven and twelve carry names such as Kidsmetics and Fun 'n Fresh so that youngsters will respond to a product specially designed for them. They also are packaged in containers that picture cartoon characters or graphics that appeal to youngsters. The primary purpose of such packaging is to provide a medium for a sales pitch.

DIRECT MAIL AND TELEMARKETING

"Hey, You at the Newsstand. Don't miss our really interesting story on THE JUNK MAIL EXPLOSION!" was the sales pitch on the cover of a recent edition of *Time* magazine. A magazine cover is another type of packaging used to try to motivate people to buy, and in the case of *Time*, the cover also was an attempt to call attention to one more way of marketing: direct mail, or selling goods and services by mail.

According to the magazine's cover story, each year advertisers mail out a total of nearly four million tons of catalogs, flyers, brochures, letters, and other printed material to tens of millions of Americans. Because a lot of the material is not wanted and is thrown out as trash, direct-mail pieces have become known as "junk mail."[11]

Yet many consumers respond to direct-mail advertising and to materials sent out by thousands of nonprofit organizations that solicit funds. Political groups and candidates for public office also seek support through mail campaigns. In all, unsolicited marketing materials sent through the mail total about 63 billion pieces per year.

Direct-mail marketing has been expanding ever since the late 1800s when first Montgomery Ward and then Richard Sears developed mail-order businesses. The Sears mail-order company began almost by chance when Richard Sears was working as a railroad agent. He received a shipment of watches but no one claimed the package, so Sears wrote to the manufacturer of the watches, offering to sell them. Sears sold all of the watches and ordered more. He then began advertising in weekly newspapers and farm magazines and sent letters and postcards describing his watches directly to potential customers. Out of 8,000 post cards mailed, he received 2,000 orders.

Sears's successful direct-mail advertising through post cards attracted the interest of A.C. Roebuck, and in 1893, Sears, Roebuck and Company was established. The company's catalogs depicting a variety of farm and household products were used primarily by people living far from department stores or other major retail stores. Families could shop by filling out an order blank and mailing it to the company, and the products were mailed to customers.

The business quickly expanded to become a vast enterprise that encompassed many department stores across the country as well as the mail-order service. In fact, Sears, Roebuck and Montgomery Ward were so successful that they prompted the formation of many other mail-order businesses. These businesses in turn have taken a large share of sales, although the Sears catalog still generates about $4 billion annually, more than any other mail-order firm.[12]

Over the past decade, direct-mail marketing has not only dramatically increased but also has become highly personalized. Because advertisers have access to computerized lists of potential customers, they can address mail to individuals, not just to a "current resident." If you receive mail addressed to you by name, you may be more responsive, more willing to see what an advertiser offers for sale or what a nonprofit organization wants you to support.

You might also be prompted to look over the contents of direct-mail advertising that comes in an envelope several times larger or more colorful than most junk mail. Or you are apt to open an envelope that has a message such as "Urgent" or "Reply Requested" or "Free Gift!" or "Win $5 Million."

Does direct-mail marketing generate responses? According to marketing firms, some 92 million Americans ordered goods and services in response to direct-mail ads sent out in 1989. That was an increase of 32 million over orders received in 1984.[13]

Telemarketing—selling by telephone—is another kind of direct marketing that is designed to get your attention immediately. Telemarketers, who work for advertisers, call consumers and try to sell everything from baby products to burial services. Some telemarketing is done by computer programs, however. Phone numbers previously entered into computer data banks are automatically dialed, and once someone answers the ringing phone, a computer-activated voice recording gives the sales pitch.

Telemedia advertising also is connected with print ads and TV commercials. For example, an ad for *Sports Illustrated* magazine listed a 900 number that readers could call to get sports scores, lineups of teams, and other sports information. Anyone making a 900 call paid the long distance charges, and the magazine enhanced its reputation with readers. In addition, the magazine was able to obtain data on callers who would be potential customers for goods and services advertised in the magazine.

Another telemedia campaign was sponsored by the soft drink company Pepsi-Cola to increase name-brand recognition among teenagers. The company advertised a 900-HOT-ROCK Trivia Game and Rock 'n' Roll Gossip Line in print and MTV commercials. Callers paid ninety-five cents per minute per call, in effect paying for the company's promotional campaign while also paying to play the game or to hear the latest music-world gossip.

WHY SOME MARKETING STRATEGIES FAIL

Several of the strategies used by advertisers and promotional experts to market their products, services, or causes have been described. But not all of these tactics work. In some cases, advertising campaigns fail to persuade large numbers of consumers because the goods or services being advertised are not what consumers want.

One prime example is the advertising campaign that the Coca Cola company used to promote New Coke, an "improved" version of its ninety-nine-year-old soft drink. According to newspaper and magazine reports, the company spent $70 million in 1985 to try to persuade consumers to buy the new product. But consumers who enjoyed the original version of the product were not convinced and demanded that the company put the old Coke back on the market.

The old Coke was indeed restored—as Coke Classic. It outsold New Coke in 1985 and the following years. Christoper Warden, contributing editor to *Consumers' Research*, explained that in 1986

Coca Cola spent $37.1 million promoting the new product, compared with $19.8 million on Coke Classic. Yet the new version garnered only 2.4% of the market to Coke Classic's 19.5%! By 1987, New Coke drinkers numbered only 1.7% of the soft-drink market to Classic Coke's 19.8%. This, despite spending well over $100 million in advertising the new product.[14]

There are many other examples of how consumer preferences and choices diminish the effects of advertising campaigns. Though highly touted and promoted, various kinds of food products, computers, games, and other kinds of goods have not sold well when consumers have not wanted or needed them or could not afford them.

There is another reason why advertising may fail to carry out its persuasive mission. According to Richard A. Feinberg, director of the Purdue (University) Retail Institute, which tracks consumer and retail trends, most advertising is not as effective as is commonly believed, because it does not tell consumers what they want to know or is not presented in a form that appeals.

One example would be using posters to advertise a literacy program; the potential consumer who does not know how to read might not get the message. Effective advertising, Feinberg maintains, uses a form or medium that reaches the audience to whom the message is targeted. More importantly, an effective ad gives consumers the information they need to make buying decisions.[15]

Marketing expert Hunter Hastings agrees that more and more consumers want factual information about products, not imagery, particularly those consumers over forty years old. These buyers look for information on a package or seek recommendations from peers or respected authorities in determining what goods and services they will purchase.[16]

Information and consumer preference along with economic factors certainly help determine buying decisions. But psychological and social factors are also at work, and knowledge of those factors may be used by advertising professionals to create messages that try to persuade people to buy.

CHAPTER FOUR

WHY WE BUY

Most of us have responded at one time or another to a type of advertising that offers a bonus, something extra along with what we buy, such as the prize in the Cracker Jack box or the special novelty inside a cereal package, or a pen attached to a common household product. Sometimes a bonus is a "twofer" item: buy one package of doughnuts and you get a duplicate package free of charge. Or perhaps the bonus is a discount on the price of a service such as a car wash. Another kind of bonus is an offer to exchange a certain number of product labels or receipts of purchase for a T-shirt, hat, pin, poster, book, or other "gift."

Such bonuses are not gifts, however. Usually, the cost of a prize or premium is added to the price charged for a product or service. Or the bonus offered might be a kind of bait designed to lure consumers into a place of business.

The "free gift" or bonus offer is just one of many motivating forces behind people's buying decisions. Of course many buying decisions are determined by basic survival needs such as food and shelter. People also need to be safe, so they may buy car seats to protect babies, for example, or insurance to cover the loss of property if there is a fire or other disaster, or a security system for a car or home to guard against robbery. Some purchases like vitamins and medications fulfill health needs. But beyond satisfying these so-called primary needs, people buy goods and services to satisfy what some psychologists have termed higher needs. These include the need to be loved, to belong, and to feel a sense of importance, power, accomplishment, or achievement.

BUYING TO SATISFY PERSONAL NEEDS

Advertisers try to convince people that buying certain goods and services will help fulfill their higher needs. Since one of those needs is the desire to be part of a group, advertisers frequently develop ads and commercials suggesting that certain products will ensure friendship or acceptance by a group.

Suppose you need a watch. Any watch that runs would fulfill the need to keep track of the hours and minutes. But print ads or TV commercials may convince you that a designer watch is what "everybody" wears, so you may decide to buy a designer watch because, among other reasons, it is a way to show that you "belong."

People not only need to feel a sense of belonging, but many also like to be part of a group having fun together. As a result, ads for soft drinks, beer, snack foods, jeans, and sneakers, for example, usually show the product being used by a group of people who are talking, laughing, and enjoying each other's company.

Services as well as products may be advertised to show they fulfill the need to be associated with a caring or fun-loving group. Ads for AT&T show family members or friends gathered for a celebration, then calling long-distance to "reach out and touch someone," a slogan that has been used successfully to convince people to choose the company's long-distance telephone service.

Even though people need to associate with others, they also like to be independent at times. Countless goods and services are advertised as a means of fulfilling the need to be distinctive. Perhaps you buy a particular kind of hat because it is different from what others own and makes you stand out in a crowd. Or you might have a car or motor scooter or bike customized so that you can express your uniqueness. Or maybe you have your hair styled so that you can show you have a special identity.

Sex appeal is another strong motivating force. Advertisers frequently try to convince consumers that buying a particular brand of shampoo, cologne, toothpaste, jeans, or car will make them more physically appealing to others. Print ads and TV commercials may show people in romantic situations or poses suggesting intimate physical contact to give the impression that using a product will help a person attract a date or a mate.

Another motivating force at work is the need to nurture, to care for others, helping them to grow and develop. For some people nurturing also means caring for pets and plants. Such motivations are taken into account by advertisers of products ranging from antiseptics to pet foods to yard-care equipment.

Several decades ago, Bactine antiseptic was developed to replace a product like iodine that cleanses a wound but may cause pain when applied. Bactine has been advertised for years as a first-aid product that has "no sting" and "no stain." Parents may be motivated to buy such a product because they can satisfy their need to comfort their children with a soothing antiseptic, as well as cleanse a cut or scratch to prevent infection.

Another first-aid product designed with nurturing in mind is the adhesive bandage. Several companies produce bandage strips printed with popular characters such as the Muppets or Teenage Mutant Ninja Turtles. The bandages are advertised to appeal to young children and also to parents, who use the colorful strips to direct their children's attention away from the hurt of cuts and scratches. After they are applied, the bandages may call attention to an injury and evoke sympathy for the hurt youngster, thus helping to satisfy the need to be comforted.

Some products for adults fulfill similar needs. TV commercials for cough syrups, pain killers, remedies for stomach upsets, and similar products show sick people getting relief from their pain or illness with the help of a product, sometimes offered by a comforting person.

To satisfy the need for achievement, people may buy sports equipment, building tools, or other products that will help them accomplish special feats. They may turn to advertising to get information about such products. Suppose a biker wants to compete in a race. She or he not only would be motivated to buy a racing bike, helmet, and similar gear, but perhaps would buy a variety of tools to maintain the bike. Or maybe the biker would be prompted to buy exercise equipment to help her or him stay in good physical condition.

Some buying decisions are prompted by the need to show status or power. Cars have long been status symbols. Ads for luxury-type cars are geared for people who want to show they have achieved wealth and/or fame and have a prominent place in society. Homes, jewelry, some types of clothing, and other goods that can be displayed may also be advertised to associate them with splendor.

People are motivated to buy some goods and services because they want to be informed or to be amused. That might be the reason for buying a book, magazine, game, computer, radio, TV, video casette player, ticket to a concert or play, or materials for a hobby or craft.

It would be impossible to describe all the different motives for buying a particular product or service. You may have learned from experience or from ads or other sources of information that certain products will suit your needs. Or you may decide to spend your money on products or services simply because they are well known. "What each of us does when we make a purchase decision depends a lot on both our personal mentality and on our social situation," wrote the authors of *Why They Buy*.[1] In short, each person buys for her or his own set of reasons.

BUYING A NAME

If you went to a supermarket with a list of products described only by such terms as gelatin dessert, paper tissues, hard candies, bandages, artificial sweetner, or soft drink, you might select from a variety of different brands, or from names given to products. But it is more likely that your list would include products known by their brand names, such as: Jell-O, Kleenex, Life Savers, Band-Aids, Sweet'n Low, Coke.

A brand name or symbol is also called a trademark, and its ownership is legally recorded, as shown by a registered trademark symbol:®. Registered brand names or symbols legally may be used only by the companies or individuals who own them.

Not all trademarks become so well known that people automatically associate products with them. But advertisers spend hundreds of millions of dollars to link a brand or company name with not only a product or service but also with an image of quality. Consumers are apt to buy what is familiar and what is seen as top-notch value.

Brand names and symbols are important factors in prompting people to choose among similar products and services. Name and symbol recognition have been responsible in part for the widespread popularity of such fast-food restaurants as McDonald's, Pizza Hut, Kentucky Fried Chicken, Burger King, and Long John Silvers, and some low-priced motel chains like Days Inn and Motel 6.

Sometimes advertisers have developed brand recognition by choosing a name that reflects what the product is or does. Kool-Aid fits the idea of a cool drink, for example, Brawny exemplifies a strong towel, Eveready suggests a battery that will hold its power, Post-It describes what can be done with self-adhesive note paper.

Slogans, repeated over and over, help bring images and names of goods and services to mind. Consider these:

"Let your fingers do the walking."

"We run the tightest ship in the shipping business."

"When it rains it pours."

"Squeezably soft."

"When you care enough to send the very best."

"Fly the friendly skies."

Another way advertisers develop name-recognition is to connect caricature-type figures with their products. "Mr. Clean," the "Jolly Green Giant," and the "Doughboy" are examples. Many products, especially those developed for children, are linked with comic strip or animated cartoon characters to help kids remember brand names.

In some instances, the names of products or services become widely known because they are advertised or endorsed by celebrities. Perhaps people buy a soft drink because they like the popular singer who appears in a commercial for the beverage. Others might buy a brand of sporting goods because they want to identify with the famous athlete whose name appears on clothing or equipment. Some consumers could be motivated to buy certain brands of tires or motor oil because movie stars and race car drivers endorse them.

When a trademark or brand name is well known, it may be used to launch new items. Such was the case with the Arm & Hammer brand name and the logo—a bent arm with hammer in hand—which long have been associated with baking soda, a product widely used as a leavening agent in baked goods. In the past, many people also used baking soda, mixed with water, to brush their teeth. Baking soda has also been used as a household cleanser, freshener, and deodorizer.

A few years ago, the company developed dental-care products with the familiar Arm & Hammer trademark on the package. Consumers recognized the trademark, associated the new dental-care products with cleansing, and were prompted to buy.

Since it costs $50 million or more to introduce a new product, many manufacturers are trying to cut back on such expenses by expanding their regular line of products with reformulated or repackaged products. This has been the case with several manufacturers of breakfast foods, who over the past few years have added oat bran or cinnamon or dried fruit or nuts to an original cereal product. They then promote the variations, or spinoffs as they are called, as new products. Companies count on name recognition to sell their spinoffs.

One product variation introduced in 1990 was Life Savers Holes, which look as if they are punched out of a roll of Life Savers. But no holes are punched from Life Savers when they are made. (Instead, a soft sugary mixture is formed around a rod, creating a hole.) The Holes are essentially the same type of candy found in a roll of Life Savers, and the two products sell for the same price. But a package of Holes contains only half the amount of candy as a roll of Life Savers.[2]

DOES ADVERTISING MANIPULATE CONSUMERS?

Along with buying to satisfy needs or to identify with the well known, people also make decisions about purchases based on such factors as their age, gender, occupation, and role in the family. What people buy may be determined as well by where they live, what they can afford or are willing to spend, and what they value. Marketing analysts and advertisers study all of these factors and more. The more knowledge that accumulates about how spending decisions are made, the more that knowledge can be used to develop advertising that may motivate consumers to purchase a particular product or service.

For years there have been debates over whether all the

information collected about consumers somehow manipulates them to buy. One of those debates has centered on subliminal advertising, the kind of ads that may appear in a subtle form, such as an image of a product that flashes on a screen for one half a second or less during a movie or TV show. Or the image might be incorporated into a magazine or other printed ad.

The term subliminal advertising also has been applied to advertising images that attempt to associate a product or service with a good feeling. And some consumers have suggested that there is a subliminal effect when they hear advertising on the radio or TV (jingles, for example) while involved in another activity; listeners are not paying attention to the ads but may mentally record some of the messages conveyed.

Apparently, concerns about subliminal advertising stem from past studies by experimental psychologists who developed theories suggesting that human behavior could be changed by messages people receive at a subconscious level; the messages, although not actually heard or seen, still register in the brain. Many self-help audio tapes have been developed and sold on the belief that the underlying directive in the tapes can change a habit or control some other aspect of personal conduct.

The idea that subliminal perception could be applied effectively in advertising has been perpetuated by a story (some say a myth) of the late 1950s. At that time, the owner of a movie theater in New Jersey flashed the words "Eat Popcorn" and "Buy Coca Cola" on the screen during a newsreel. The owner claimed that the messages increased sales of popcorn by nearly 58 percent and Coke by 18 percent. But since then no experiment under controlled conditions has been able to replicate such results. Although a few advertisers claim that subliminal suggestions help sell products, most marketing and advertising professionals dismiss the idea as fantasy. And even if hidden messages were effective sales tools, advertisers are prohibited by law from using them.[3]

Another controversy focuses on advertising aimed at young children. Some consumer groups argue that advertising places pressure on young children who do not have the skills or knowledge to distinguish between factual information and hype, or exaggeration, in ads. The critics say that from a very early age youngsters are being conditioned to consume more and more but are not being taught how to make wise consumer choices.

One simplified example of this process might be a youngster who, over and over again, sees many TV commercials for snack foods. The commercials continually show the foods in connection with people or cartoon characters having fun, enjoying good health, brimming with happiness. A young viewer associates health and happiness with the foods, even though the snack foods have little or no nutritious value and are high in calories. The association may also help establish a life-long habit of consuming too many fatty foods that contribute to poor health.

Those who rebut such an argument say that parents, not advertisers, are responsible for helping children develop healthy eating habits as well as other positive life skills. According to their view, concerned parents ought to take the initiative to learn about the products advertised on TV and in other media and then guide their children in making wise buying decisions.

One more debate over the influence of advertising centers on whether or not ads create unrealistic expectations. Some advertising critics argue that many printed ads and radio and TV commercials imply that you have to drive car A and wear products B and C to demonstrate success, and consume products D and E to be popular. You also have to use products F and G to show that you are of some worth. Such implied messages, day in and day out, may create dissatisfactions, and people who are unable to afford products A, B, C, D, E, F, and G may think they have little value as individuals.

In a recent book on advertising, Carol Moog, a clinical psychologist and marketing researcher, explains how one of her clients, whom she called Marlene, tried to measure up to the images of seductive women shown in printed ads and TV commercials:

> When [Marlene] was a teenager, she thought she was ugly, that no boy would ever like her. She wanted to be beautiful and seductive . . . she used ads directly, deliberately, to teach herself how to look sexy . . . she'd practice holding her lips in the open, pouty way models do when they sell makeup, or arching her back to push out her chest, or bending over to show off her rear like she saw in all the jean ads . . .
>
> Marlene's grown older, but the images on the commercials haven't, and she's still measuring herself against them. She sees the young, flirtatious, sexy couples . . . [but] the gap between the images and her reality has widened . . .

According to Moog, Marlene believed her marriage was failing, although her husband had never indicated any dissatisfaction. Marlene's belief stemmed from how she compared herself and her husband with sexy couples shown in advertising. She expected the ads to show her "how to act and who to be, in order to get love." Marlene was still trying "to create herself in the image of magazine models."[4]

On the other hand, advertisers might say that Marlene's actions simply reflect values and attitudes already present in society. Whatever the content of the advertising, they argue, most ads primarily provide information about goods and services that are available in the marketplace. Without that information, people would not be able to find and buy what they need. Consuming goods and services in turn keeps businesses, manufacturing plants, and service industries operating, providing jobs, and raising living standards for most of the population.

Some economists point out that advertising is essential not only to promote economic growth but also to maintain high-quality goods and services at reasonable prices. In one study, for example, economists found that when the Mattel Toy Company began in the 1950s to advertise one of its products—a $5.00 toy—on television, the price of the toy dropped to $3.50 in cities where TV advertising was frequent and sales were brisk. But in cities where there was little or no advertising, the price of the toy remained at about $4.95.[5]

Yet the price of a product or service is not the only factor to consider when determining the effects of advertising. Perhaps a young viewer has never thought about buying a particular toy. If TV advertising presents the toy in a way that appeals to a youngster, is that youngster being influenced by the commercial? Is the ad creating a "want," or demand, that was not there before?

Probably there will always be debates over advertising's influence and how advertisers use knowledge about human behavior to try to sell goods and services. However, consumers can make prudent choices if they are aware of the ways that advertising sometimes implies that certain things will fulfill hopes, dreams, or fantasies or will help a person achieve popularity, status, or power.

Knowing what can prompt you to buy is a first step toward determining whether you really need or want a particular product or service and whether you can afford to pay for it. Of course, for many everyday purchases, little or no analysis of why you buy is necessary. Usually, you follow an established routine, buying and replenishing basic supplies. But if you make a practice of learning about the options available in the marketplace and then buy goods and services that fit your needs, your life-style, and your budget, you are not likely to be manipulated by selling techniques.

Nevertheless, advertisers will continue to aim ads and commercials your way. In fact, you are likely to be part of a specific group—a so-called target group—that advertisers hope to reach. Marketing goods and services toward target groups is one more way that advertisers try to sell their goods and services.

CHAPTER FIVE

ADVERTISING AIMED AT TARGET GROUPS

Young children between the ages of 4 and 12 in the United States represent a market for an estimated $75 billion worth of goods and services each year, most of which are purchased by adults.[1]

Teenagers spend at least $55 billion annually on consumer goods and services, ranging from automobiles to groceries.[2]

College students spend a total of about $20 billion on purchases other than those directly connected with their education, such as the cost of tuition, books, and housing.[3]

With billions of dollars at stake, it is no wonder that advertisers search for and often find ways to target these particular groups with sales pitches. But these groups are not the only ones that advertisers try to reach.

Some advertisers gear their messages toward people in specific ethnic groups, such as African-Americans or Hispanics. Other advertisers target people in certain professions or occupations, placing ads in special magazines directed to teachers, doctors, writers, artists, engineers, homemakers, salespeople, truckers, or other groups. Many ads are designed for people who enjoy a particular hobby or leisure activity, such as bird watching, hunting, stamp collecting, or woodworking.

Other target groups for advertisers may be people who are nutrition conscious, or concert-goers, or animal lovers, or travelers, or sports fans. The list could go on and on. The fact is, companies not only appeal to broad market groups, such as teenagers, but also try to narrow their marketing to groups within groups, such as teenagers who own cars. As marketing experts have pointed out, goods and services and advertisements for them are designed to "fit" specific groups, because that is the most economical and effective way to spend advertising dollars.

However, some consumer and environmental organizations, sociologists, educators, and others are concerned that targeted advertising encourages people to greater and greater levels of consumption when, they argue, conservation of limited resources and reuse of goods could be more beneficial to society. Some also are concerned that a heavy bombardment of advertising may unduly influence a targeted group such as young children who do not have the information, experience, or sophistication they need to adequately analyze advertising messages.

SELLING KIDSTUFF

Many types of businesses—from discount stores to comic book publishers to TV and radio broadcasters—consider the 32 million American children between the ages of four and twelve a viable market for a variety of products and services. Although adults make most purchases for youngsters, some purchases are made by children who have gift or allowance money to spend. Both children and their parents spend an estimated total amount of $9 billion annually.[4]

According to marketing professor James McNeal, kids buy snacks, candies, and other sweets, as well as toys and games. Depending on the children's age, toy characters linked with cartoon or comic strip characters (Batman and Dick Tracy, for example), dolls, and video games are popular items. Young children also spend millions of dollars in arcades and at the movies. They buy $760 million worth of clothing, much of which carries the trademarks of TV personalities or famous athletes.[5]

Such products, along with breakfast cereals and soft drinks, are promoted frequently through TV commercials. Consumers Union, a nonprofit organization that conducts research on the quality of products and services, estimates that each year 30,000 TV ads are beamed at young children. Advertisers spend from $450 million to about $500 million each year to create these commercials, which usually are aired during children's programs on weekends or during after-school hours.[6]

Advertisers use other means of reaching children, some of them fairly recent innovations. Retail stores, for example, have set up activity rooms where young children can play while their parents shop. How does such an activity influence kids to buy? Frequently, youngsters play with toys and games or watch videos that are for sale in the stores, particularly in department stores like Sears, which teamed up with McDonald's to set up McKids activity rooms. The McKids sign over a special entrance for kids, which is no more than 4 feet (1.21m) high, carries the familiar golden arches trademark, helping to reinforce the name and prompting kids to buy at McDonald's as well as at Sears.

Many promotional activities such as poster contests and spelling bees bring school-age children and their families into stores to buy products that kids want. Special promotions such as talent shows, Halloween costume parades, and the annual arrival of Santa Claus are used at shopping centers and malls to entice youngsters and their families to buy.

Kid clubs are popping up in all kinds of places to appeal to so-called "tweens" (namely, children between the ages of seven and twelve) who are potential consumers. Children's clubs have been popular since the radio programs of the 1930s when young fans of Little Orphan Annie, Captain Midnight, and Jolly Joe eagerly bought the products advertised on these programs and sent in box tops or labels from food products to become club members.

During the 1950s, the "Mickey Mouse Club" TV show was popular nationwide with young viewers, many of whom sprouted Mickey Mouse ears (special hats) or bought other Disney products. Although the Mickey Mouse Club faded from the scene for a while, it is now back in a new format, complete with Mickey Mouse ears in flashy neon lights!

Other clubs are set up by TV networks as well as by fast-food restaurants, food packagers, game manufacturers, compact disc and tape companies, and magazine publishers. A few clubs are free, but to join most clubs, kids have to send in proof-of-purchase seals from products and/or mail in annual club dues, which pay for club newsletters or magazines, T-shirts, badges, and discount coupons for other products or services. *Zillions*, a consumer magazine for kids published by Consumers Union, noted that some of their readers believed kids clubs are a "rip off" and just want young people to buy.[7]

Although companies spend about $500,000 to set up a club, one of the most important returns for advertisers is the consumer information they receive. When kids join clubs, the forms they fill out become part of a data base that can be used to direct ever more products and advertising their way. Clubs also help establish name recognition and perhaps life-long loyalty for a company or product.[8]

STUDENTS AS TARGETS

It has been commonly believed that schools are free of advertising. But many educational materials sponsored by corporations carry ads or promote the use of certain products. Some examples: Polaroid provides schools with educational materials that include the company name and also offer schools a "free" camera in exchange for ten proof-of-purchase symbols from Polaroid film. Chef Boy-ar-Dee has distributed cookbooks to schools; some of the recipes call for the company's products, which of course is a form of promotion.

Some companies contribute funds to schools in return for box tops and labels from packaged goods, which thus encourages young people and adults to buy the products. Campbell's provides schools with sports equipment in exchange for soup labels, and PepsiCo donates sports equipment and other items when allowed to place their vending machines in schools.

These and other practices that target some 20 million students, or about half the U.S. school population, have been widely criticized. In a recent report called *Selling America's Kids*, Consumers Union charges that advertisers exploit kids by planting advertising messages in schools. As Charlotte Baecher, editor of *Zillions,* explained, companies that provide schools with so-called learning tools often provide materials that are self-serving and that contain biased information. "When a commercial message is delivered in school, it's an implicit endorsement. And kids aren't likely to question a commercial embedded in a lesson," Baecher said.[9]

However, some advertisers say they are acting responsibly and that many schools ask for their help with a variety of projects. Companies say they provide teaching materials that some schools and teachers cannot afford to buy. AT&T, for example, sponsors a science magazine that covers the communication industry and its impact on daily life. Discover Card (a credit card company) sponsors an annual financial magazine aimed at high school students. According to a report in *AdWeek*, a magazine for advertisers, a company's "presence is marked by nothing more than a logo identification," but the advertisers admit this is a way to reach the target audience and to develop awareness of brand names.[10]

One of the most controversial forms of advertising targeted for students is a TV news channel called Channel One. Although schools like the idea of presenting current events to teenagers, Channel One includes two minutes of advertising in its 12-minute newscast. The cable network CNN also offers a newscast ("Newsroom") that is channeled to thousands of schools, but includes no advertising during its 15-minute program. Several other cable channels and the Public Broadcasting Service provide a variety of educational TV programs for students as well. The major difference with Channel One is that it was designed with advertising in mind by Whittle Communications, a Knoxville, Tennessee, company that specializes in targeted advertising.

Christopher Whittle, creator of the concept, says his cable TV show is a perfect way to teach current affairs, since teenagers seldom read about or listen to newscasts describing local, national, and world events that can affect their lives. Schools that agree to subscribe to Channel One and to show the program daily to 90 percent of their students receive free TV sets, usually one for each classroom, and also VCRs and satellite dishes. These are attractive bait for many schools that cannot afford to buy such electronic equipment. Whittle Communications's advertising fees—$300,000 per minute of air time in 1990—pays for the news program and the video equipment.[11]

Thousands of schools across the nation have signed up for Channel One broadcasts. Some educators believe that it is important to have the free TV equipment in order to present the news to students. The newscast can initiate discussions about current events and can be integrated into social studies lessons. Ironically, teachers also can use the commercials to develop critical thinking about advertising in general, helping students to see, for example, how sexuality pervades many ads, and to learn how to be wise consumers.

But many parents and members of school boards and education groups object to Channel One newscasts, and some states have passed laws banning the program. They argue that the advertising in the TV program is directed specifically at a captive audience. Students have no choice in whether they will watch the commercials interspersed with the newscast. Critics also say the news program is superficial, merely skimming the surface of important issues. There are fears, too, that news from only one source could manipulate student attitudes and views. Another concern is that students already spend too much time watching TV, and teachers might add to the problem if they rely on video programs to teach rather than teaching lessons themselves.

THE TEENAGE MARKET

Whether commercials are directed at teenagers in or out of school classrooms, there is little doubt that advertisers want to reach the 28 million consumers between the ages of twelve and nineteen who have at least $55 billion to spend each year. Not only do teenagers buy such common items as fast foods, soft drinks, snacks, music tapes, and videos, but at least 80 percent of teenagers are "heavily involved" in the weekly grocery shopping for their families. As a result, food packagers have developed products that appeal to teenage consumers. Teenagers also help determine the purchase each year of billions of dollars worth of products such as TV sets, tape recorders, motor scooters, cars, sports equipment, clothing, and many other high-priced items.[12]

How do advertisers reach the teenage market? One way is through TV commercials broadcast on MTV and other cable channels aimed primarily at thirteen to nineteen year olds. Another method used to reach teenagers is placing products in movies. Advertisers pay huge sums to have their products prominently shown in films, giving the impression that stars are endorsing the products and reinforcing brand-name recognition.

Another method of targeting the teen group is through special events such as concerts, auto racing, and athletic competitions. Advertisers also capitalize on transition periods in the lives of young people. Before the school prom, for example, businesses target teenagers and their parents with sales pitches for goods and services ranging from elegant gowns, flowers, tuxedo rentals and cummerbunds to limousine service, restaurants, and entertainment after the prom.

One advertising campaign that has developed recently plays on a girl's rite of passage into womanhood. Called the "Sweet 16" campaign, it attempts to link diamonds to a girl's sixteenth birthday celebration. Since diamonds have not been considered a teenage product and traditionally have been purchased for engagements, anniversaries, and similar events, the strategy of the "Sweet 16" campaign is to motivate girls to ask their parents to buy diamond jewelry as birthday gifts or to establish the idea in parents' minds.

TARGETING DRINKERS AND SMOKERS

In spite of the fact that a primary cause of death among young people aged sixteen to twenty-four is traffic accidents related to drinking alcoholic beverages, many advertisers of beer and liquor appear to aim their messages at this target group. Campaigns and laws against selling alcoholic beverages to minors apparently have little effect on stemming the ads for these products, although the liquor industry voluntarily restricts advertising on radio and TV. But the industry uses other media and sponsors special events such as art tours, festivals, parades, dances, athletic competitions, and car racing to promote its products.

Beer companies legally can advertise their products in a variety of media and for many years have conducted promotional campaigns during the annual spring break—the time when high school and college students gather at resort cities in Florida and in the Southwest. The promotions at Daytona Beach, Florida, during one recent spring season were typical. There were the usual print ads and billboards for beer. In addition, one of the brewers set up a huge inflatable six-pack on the beach to advertise its brand, gave away T-shirts and hats, and another brewer opened a center where students could get free breakfasts. Beer sold for only twenty-five cents a can at some taverns, and one advertising sign outside a bar suggested that students "Party 'Til You Puke," according to a report in the *Washington Post*.[13]

At other times of the year, beer brewers sponsor a variety of special events that draw young crowds. For example, one study by the Marin Institute in San Rafael, California, found that brewers spend about $50 million each year to sponsor drag and stock car racing and monster truck derbies across the nation. These events, the institute noted, are largely attended by teenage males, a group with the highest incidence of drunk driving. The California researchers believe that beer companies sponsoring motor sports are encouraging teenagers to drink by "sending the message that alcohol and fast driving mix." The study group would like to see such advertising at motor sports banned.[14]

Groups against alcohol abuse have made similar complaints about beer companies that sponsor athletic competitions or music concerts. In opposing such sponsorship, critics charge that beer companies are looking for new customers among the teenage and young adult groups. Beer companies deny the charges, saying their advertising is aimed only at people who legally may drink alcoholic beverages and that they are trying to create a brand preference. In addition, beer companies say they have developed campaigns to promote what they call "responsible drinking."

The tobacco industry also has been berated for its advertising, which appeals to young people by making smoking look glamorous or look like a "fun" thing to do. Like the alcohol industry, tobacco companies sponsor sporting events to promote their products, which could suggest to young people that smoking is a healthy pastime. Soon after Dr. Louis W. Sullivan was appointed the U.S. secretary of health and human services, he denounced sports figures who promote smoking and called on professional athletes to reject sponsorship of "a product, that when used as intended, causes death."[15]

Over the past few years many health groups, political leaders, educators, and others in the United States have intensified their attacks on cigarette advertising that plays on teenagers' desire for independence as well as appealing to their need to be sexually attractive and accepted socially. There also have been protests against cigarette ads that use cartoon characters such as Old Joe, the dapper camel in Camel cigarette advertising, designed to appeal to young people.[16]

Tobacco industry spokespeople say that advertising does not compel teenagers to smoke since, according to one industry representative, ads do not tout marijuana and kids still smoke it. Cigarette manufacturers argue that they are advertising for their share of the market, appealing to those who already smoke or want to smoke.

Statistics show that many Americans have given up the smoking habit. One example: only about 30 percent of those in their early twenties smoke today, compared to the 1960s when about 60 percent of males and over 40 percent of females in that age group smoked. But smoking has increased substantially among teenagers, especially girls and members of minority groups.

Mark Green, Commissioner of the New York City Department of Consumer Affairs, put it this way:

> Each day the merchants of nicotine lose more than five thousand customers who either die or quit. To replace these lost customers, the tobacco industry spends billions to hook kids on cigarettes—since they know that half of all adult smokers started smoking by age 13, and that a full one-quarter started by age 11.[17]

Well-known columnist George Will wrote even harsher words:

> Tobacco companies bring a chilly clarity to the task of coping with a shrinking market. They use sophisticated marketing like a sniper's rifle, drawing beads on the most vulnerable, manipulable Americans. The rate of smoking is two-and-a-half times as high among Americans who have not finished high school as among college graduates.[18]

For many years, alcohol and tobacco companies have been aiming their advertising at other target groups, particularly blacks and Hispanics. But health officials and some community leaders have begun to criticize some targeted ad campaigns. For example, when R.J. Reynolds (RJR) tried to market a new cigarette called Uptown to blacks, U.S. Health and Human Services Secretary Sullivan blasted the product and the ad campaign. Dr. Sullivan pointed out that blacks as a group already smoke more than whites and have a lung cancer rate 58 percent higher than that of whites. As other black leaders aired similar complaints and criticisms, the tobacco company decided not to launch its new product and canceled its advertising campaign, although no one is sure whether or not this is a permanent decision.

RJR reportedly plans to target another group with a cigarette called Dakota. At first, it was geared for young women between the ages of eighteen and twenty-four, many of whom work in factories. One marketing agency called the target group "virile females" and suggested that the cigarette be linked to such events as drag racing that the women attend with their boyfriends. Women's groups and health experts protested that the company was deliberately planning to encourage young women who may not be well informed to smoke and risk death from lung cancer. But the company recently said it plans to market the new cigarette to both women and men if tests show it will be popular. In fact, in late 1990, cartons of the new product were sent to members of the U.S. armed forces for sampling.

Other disputes over tobacco and alcohol advertising have focused on billboard ads in black and Hispanic communities. Opponents of billboard ads that tout the pleasures of smoking and drinking say that such ads are more often placed in inner-city minority communities than in predominantly Anglo neighborhoods or white suburban areas, a charge that billboard companies refute. Some church congregations in New York's predominantly black Harlem community began a campaign to cover the billboards with white paint. Although such actions are illegal, they have been repeated in other cities.

In Chicago, a man who called himself Mandrake and described himself as a black professional, told an Associated Press reporter that he was responsible for whitewashing billboards on the city's South Side, a predominantly black neighborhood. Mandrake said he understood he was vandalizing private property and breaking the law, but that he considered his actions civil disobedience. He said "it was time to stand up and fight back" against the "disproportionate amount of [alcohol and tobacco] advertising in the black and Hispanic community."[19]

On the other hand, some minority businesses and organizations are concerned that if tobacco and alcohol advertising dollars are not spent in minority communities, there will be few funds for cultural events and some businesses will fail. Publishers of black newspapers and magazines, for example, fear that they could go out of business without the revenues from ads placed by cigarette, beer, and liquor companies. In New York during Harlem Week, when African-American culture and achievements are highlighted, cigarette and liquor companies have paid for many of the costs, and there has been controversy among the festival organizers about whether or not to continue to accept such funds. In 1990, alcohol and tobacco companies supported some Harlem Week festivities but products were not as highly publicized as in prior years.[20]

Organizers of Hispanic festivals and owners of Hispanic businesses have wrestled with similar pressures, as has been documented in a report published by the Center for Science in the Public Interest. Titled *Marketing Disease to Hispanics*, the report points out that many companies today "are tripping over each other" trying to target their advertising for the Hispanic market, but that alcohol and tobacco industries have conducted such targeted campaigns for years. "That targeting is now starting to take its toll. Recent research shows that Hispanics are suffering from an ever-increasing number of health problems related to drinking and smoking," the authors of the report noted.[21]

Researchers, government leaders, and health officials quoted in the report emphasize that more efforts are needed to increase awareness of how advertising affects buying habits and how these are related to the adverse effects of smoking and drinking. Experts also say that more attention must be paid to economic and political issues that are closely linked to health problems in minority communities.

The goal of those concerned about protecting human life and health is to convince people not to buy legal, but addictive, drugs such as alcohol and tobacco.

ADS AIMED AT THE HEALTH-CONSCIOUS

It would seem that advertisers who promote nutritious or healthy foods are quite the opposite of advertisers who promote alcohol and tobacco. But consumers still need to be wary of advertising campaigns designed to appeal to those concerned about nutrition and their health. For a number of years, many packaged food products have carried such messages as "100% natural," "vitamin enriched," "nutritionally balanced," "high in protein," "high-fiber," "low sodium," "no cholesterol," "lite," "low-calorie," "sugar-free," "no palm oil," or "no fat."

Health-conscious people frequently look for and buy products that appear to be what they need to maintain proper diets. People who are overweight, people who have heart disease, diabetes, allergies, or other ailments, and people who try to prevent illness usually want foods that fit their specific needs. As a result they may buy packaged foods that not only carry health claims but that also have brand names that suggest good nutrition. Brands such as Healthy Choice, Lean Cuisine, and Weight Watchers are examples. But can consumers depend on what advertisers say about their food products? Sometimes, but not always.

Many packaged foods carry messages claiming that the products are rich in oat bran, a fiber that some medical studies suggest could lower blood cholesterol, fatty substances that build up in arteries and lead to strokes or other heart disease. Using findings from the studies, advertisers for such products as cereals, waffles, cookies, muffins, chips, pretzels, and even beer have designed packages that almost shouted the word "oat bran," hoping to target those wanting heart-healthy foods.

But in early 1990, a report of a study published in the

Street criers and peddlers used their own voices to advertise what they had to sell.

Displays at the American Museum of Advertising, the
first museum of its kind, in Portland, Oregon, show
a variety of ads in diverse media. Many of the ads
have historical significance and are considered
classic forms of advertising.

NATIONAL COMMITTEE TO PRESERVE
SOCIAL SECURITY AND MEDICARE
2000 K Street N.W.
Washington D.C. 20006

MR. ARTHUR L GAY
1711 E BEARDSLEY AVE
ELKHART, IN 46514

No sooner was the ink dry
on the recent
Medicare cost increases than:

"Budget Director Richard Darman...
instructed his staff to take a fresh look
at all spending programs including...
Social Security and Medicare..."

Wall Street Journal
November 16, 1990

The National Committee is independent of Congress, every government

*Above: Organizations soliciting funds
through direct-mail advertising sometimes
use oversized envelopes like this to
attract the attention of supporters.
Other advertisers use contests and
URGENT! messages (right) to entice
people to read their pitch.*

Above: Packaging, displays, and signs—these are just a few of the media used in stores to present advertising messages. Right: This letter to Santa Clause clearly shows the influence of advertising.

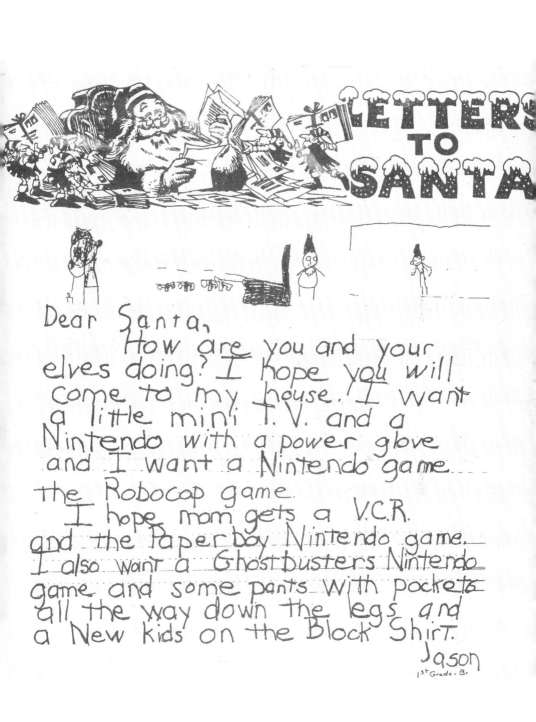

LETTERS TO SANTA

Dear Santa,
How are you and your
elves doing? I hope you will
come to my house. I want
a little mini T.V. and a
Nintendo with a power glove
and I want a Nintendo game
the Robocop game.
I hope mom gets a V.C.R.
and the Paperboy Nintendo game.
I also want a Ghostbusters Nintendo
game and some pants with pockets
all the way down the legs and
a New kids on the Block Shirt.

Jason
1st Grade - Br

*Above: Classic Burma-Shave signs hang from the ceiling
in the American Museum of Advertising in Portland.
Right: Ad agencies sometimes create campaigns
pro bono for public service advertisements.
Here, an ad in an AIDS awareness campaign
is aimed at teenagers.*

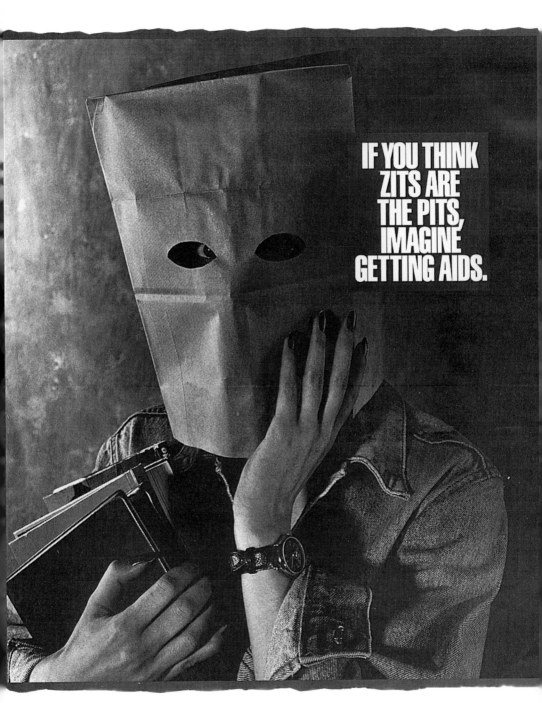

IF YOU THINK ZITS ARE THE PITS, IMAGINE GETTING AIDS.

PEOPLE UNITED AGAINST AIDS

 Don't have sex, *or* Have one sexual partner. Use condoms for safer sex.

 Don't shoot. If you do shoot, don't share rigs.

 If you share rigs, *bleach* works *between* users.

 For more information, or to volunteer, call: 223-AIDS or 1-800-777-AIDS.

Left: Celebrities such as Paul Newman have long been part of the car-racing scene. Like many other drivers, he wears uniforms with advertisements for a variety of products.
Above: Sales are common ways to attract buyers and lure them into stores.

Above: Cents-off coupons and rebates are ways that advertisers try to appeal to consumers. When the cents-off and money-back coupons are returned to advertisers, they provide information about consumer buying decisions that can be used to develop ads and promotions aimed at specific groups.
Left: A giant Paul Bunyan is used to attract attention outside a hardware store.

*A successful symbol will instantly identify a product
to consumers. Even with the clutter of signs on a
commercial street, most people are able to pick out
the familiar golden arches that identify a chain
of fast-food restaurants.*

The largest-size package may not always be the "best buy." Checking the weight or volume in a package and determining the unit price (often listed on store shelves) will indicate which package offers the most for your money.

Caution! You may be an advertisement if you wear clothes with brand names printed on them.

New England Journal of Medicine questioned whether oat bran could do much to lower cholesterol levels. Advertisers have criticized the recent study, saying it could be faulty because it was limited to people with low cholesterol levels. Many stick by earlier studies that show the health benefits of oat bran. So who should consumers believe? Health experts say that oat bran is a nutritional asset to most people's diets, but they warn that no one food will prevent or cure a disease or ailment.[22]

Because of the oat bran assertions and many other confusing or misleading health claims for foods, the U.S. Congress recently passed legislation regarding food labeling. The law requires a standard format for labels on processed foods. Labels must provide nutritional information, including calorie and cholesterol content, and indicate the amounts of salt, sugar, fats, fiber, vitamins, and minerals in the foods. Similar information must be provided for fresh foods such as raw fruits, vegetables, and fish. The U.S. secretary of health and human services is responsible for determining how such terms as "high fiber" or "low fat" can be used, and the U.S. Food and Drug Administration is responsible for setting up and enforcing guidelines for food labeling.[23]

Another food labeling quandary has developed over so-called organic foods. Because of widespread concerns about the use and effects of toxic chemical pesticides and the possible pesticide residues on fresh fruits and vegetables, there has been an increasing demand for organic foods, or foods grown without synthetic chemical pesticides and fertilizers. More than twenty states have set up standards for organic foods, but these standards vary widely and do not necessarily ban the use of all synthetic chemicals. Some certification programs have been misleading, also. Labels indicate that the foods have been certified, but they do not say what the foods have been certified for—in other words, the foods may simply have chemical residues no higher than those allowed by federal laws.

However, federal legislation passed in 1990 to provide funds for farm programs also includes provisions for organic food labeling. The law requires that any foods labeled as organically grown must meet federal standards, which are set by a federal board. Federal regulations also require that any grower who sells organic foods must register with the U.S. Department of Agriculture (USDA) and be certified by a USDA-approved agency. Another provision of the law stipulates that no processed foods such as cereal can be labeled organic unless 95 percent of the ingredients (excluding water and salt) are organic. Such regulations are expected to eliminate some of the confusion surrounding organic labeling.

Yet food label regulations by themselves are not enough to determine which foods will fulfill a person's nutritional needs. Consumers need to educate themselves about the meanings of the terms used on food labels and about which foods provide benefits. For instance, a person might want to investigate whether organically grown foods are any more nutritious than those grown the conventional way.

Cost might also be a factor. Some agricultural studies have shown that when agrichemicals (synthetic chemical pesticides and fertilizers) are reduced or eliminated, crop yields decrease. Thus the costs of food rise by about 12 percent, according to a report in *Consumers' Research.*[24]

However, a study on alternative agriculture conducted by the National Academy of Sciences found that on test farms where agrichemicals were reduced *and farms were managed efficiently* (using such practices as soil conservation and crop rotation), the yields of major crops remained about the same, or even increased in some cases. But overall, conventional farming practices in the United States depend on agrichemicals and are supported by federal farm programs. As a result, foods produced with reduced or no agrichemicals may cost more.[25]

CHAPTER SIX

TRENDS IN ADVERTISING

Whether advertisers target small specialized groups or huge population groups across the United States or in another nation, they usually present their messages in a manner and a style reflecting the times. Changes in the media, particularly in the development of electronic media such as TV and telemarketing, have determined some techniques used in advertising. Some federal and state laws and pressure from consumer groups have influenced the kinds of advertising that appear. And some advertising techniques and messages have been dictated by what the general public and advertisers consider acceptable.

OVERCOMING STEREOTYPES

The kinds of images acceptable in advertising over the years have included many stereotypes—portrayals based on fixed ideas about the traits of people who belong to a particular racial, ethnic, age, gender, or occupational groups. When advertisements have portrayed stereotypes of ethnic or racial groups, for example, the images have exaggerated traits that are considered negative, such as laziness, selfishness, greed, passiveness, and ignorance. These images have reflected views commonly held by the majority group—that is, white Anglo-Saxon Protestant Americans.[1]

Throughout history many majority groups have seen themselves as having "superior" qualities, while tending to judge members of a group different from themselves as "inferior." Since most forms of communication in the United States have been dominated for years by people of the majority group, stereotypical ideas about people of color or people of ethnic groups (including non-Christians) have appeared in print and broadcast media. Some examples: Asians have been depicted as laundry workers, Native Americans as savages, Arabs as barbarians, Mexican-Americans as bandits, Jews as greedy merchants, and Italians as criminals.

Perhaps the most long-standing stereotypes in advertising have been of blacks, who for decades were portrayed as less than human or at best buffoons or servants. Ads for Aunt Jemima pancake mix, for example, portrayed a stereotypical plantation "mammy" with a kerchief wound around her head, grinning broadly and "talking" in ad copy like an unschooled former slave. Due to protests by civil rights groups during the 1960s, the portrayals were altered somewhat to show an image of an African-American woman wearing a headband and "speaking" standard English. Today, Aunt Jemima appears as a woman of her times; the head covering is gone and she wears earrings and a stylish hairdo.[2]

Until the late 1960s, few African-Americans even appeared in print and TV advertisements or were allowed to work in the field of advertising and promotion. "Advertisers feared that blacks in ads would ruin sales, not promote products," explained the owner of a New York consulting firm that promotes minority talent for advertising. "But once companies realized that the black community was a huge market for goods and services, advertisers tried to gear ads toward that market, which meant using black Americans in ads. But white advertisers did not really understand the life-styles of blacks. I know of one company, for instance, that used clean-shaven black men in ads for its razors and blades. It was a foolish error, since for years the majority of black men have worn mustaches—and they wouldn't shave them off—which should have been obvious to even a casual observer."[3]

Portrayals of blacks and other minority groups have become more realistic as advertisers have become more aware of stereotypical attitudes and how these are propagated through advertising images. But many advertising analysts and civil rights groups believe that mainstream ads still do not adequately reflect the diversity of Americans. Although people of various ethnic groups certainly appear in ads, models in TV commercials, magazine and newspaper ads, and billboards are predominantly Anglo-Saxon. The majority of store mannequins and models used in catalogs and department store ads also are white.

John Schrag, a reporter for a weekly newspaper in Portland, Oregon, conducted a survey of retail stores in the city's downtown area during December 1990 and found that businesses were "still dreaming of a white Christmas." Schrag pointed out that it was probably not unusual for retailers in a predominantly white area to show only white models in ads. But, he wrote, "the advertisements and store displays . . . don't even reflect the small minority population of the areas they serve." Although Schrag noted that the skin colors of models and mannequins were not priority issues for members of minority groups, the preponderance of white images does send a message to people of color. As one black educator told him: "When you see an absence of people who look like you in catalogs and newspaper advertisements, it says to you, 'You're not important, people don't care about you.' I deal with children all the time, and I can assure you, kids pick up on that."[4]

Many ads also reinforce stereotypes of gender. Women in ads usually are shown pursuing roles established at the beginning of the industrial age. Before that time, men and women shared work in the fields and in home crafts. But with the advent of factories, men began to take jobs outside the home while women were expected to perform most household tasks and care for children. Today, women are not confined exclusively to home and child-care roles. The U.S. Department of Labor statistics show, for example, that about 74 percent of the women aged twenty to forty-four are in the labor force. Yet many ads do not give this impression: young women frequently are stereotyped as homemakers or sex objects.

One ad caught the attention of Ellen Goodman, syndicated columnist for the *Boston Globe*, who, in scornful fashion, bestows "Equal Rites Awards" each year on "those who have done their utmost . . . to slow the progress of women." Her 1990 advertising award went "to the folks who devised the new Lysol ad." Featuring a manicured hand on the toilet bowl, the copy reads, "With Men or Boys at Home, Your Bathroom Needs Cleaning Every Day." The ad, Goodman declared, deserves "one solid flush."[5]

Although some advertisers would argue that such an ad was designed to appeal to a target group, the fact remains that the way the message was presented was insulting to some women. The ad clearly presented the idea that cleaning the toilet is a "woman's job," an image that perpetuates a stereotype.

The age group of fifty and over, which includes at least 63 million Americans and is growing rapidly, is another market group that has been frequently stereotyped in ads. Since the group controls more than 70 percent of the nation's wealth, many manufacturers, service industries, and advertising professionals are especially interested in appealing to the fifty-plus consumers, who frequently are called "Seniors," "Golden Agers," or "Elderly," terms that most people over fifty dislike.

Although few can agree on an appropriate term, marketing expert David Wolfe, who advises many advertisers on how to sell to the fifty-plus market, describes the group as the "ageless market." He explains that contrary to popular belief, the fifty-plus group does not regret the loss of youth and is not overanxious about health problems and death. Rather, Wolfe and his research group have found that a majority of "mature older people are too involved with living life to think much about the end of life."[6]

Wolfe also emphasizes that the group includes people from all walks of life; they range from those who ride in bicycle marathons and compete in a variety of sports to people who may be in wheelchairs or have sight and hearing deficiencies. But in spite of market research, advertising practitioners too often have accepted the myths about aging and have designed ads that show older people in rocking chairs or with hearing problems or acting as if they have no vitality or interest in life.

Such stereotypes have resulted in lost sales. In one survey of older consumers, one-third of those surveyed said they deliberately refused to buy products that had been advertised in ways that stereotype or present caricatures of mature adults. Many older people also say they have been turned off by ads that stress age and pain and suffering.[7]

SIGNS OF THE TIMES

Along with protesting stereotypes in ads, some consumer groups also have been increasingly vocal about the way some advertising media are used. Billboard advertising, for example, has come under fire recently for a variety of reasons, including the charges that billboard ads for alcohol and tobacco abound in minority communities.

Another primary concern is what some individuals and public interest groups call visual blight or pollution. They would agree with the late Frank Lloyd Wright, a famous architect who noted years ago that the urban scene was a jumble of "Glaring signs . . . sharp signs. Hurrah signs. Stop signs. Come-on-in signs. Names obliterating everything. Names and what they would do for you or with you or to you for your money."[8]

Signs along roadways and painted on barns and other buildings have been used for decades to advertise. One advertising campaign using roadway signs was popular with motorists for nearly forty years. The campaign was initiated in 1925 by advertisers of Burma Shave, a shaving cream product. A series of six small wooden signs were placed one hundred feet apart along the roadway and were designed to be read at thirty-five miles per hour (56 kpm). Each sign carried part of an amusing jingle, the last one always spelling out: "Burma Shave."

One series of signs noted: "Statistics Prove / Near and Far / That Folks / Who Drive Like Crazy / Are . . . / Burma Shave." About 600 different jingles were produced and put up along America's roadways over the years. But as the speed of highway travel increased, the signs could no longer be read easily, and the campaign ended in 1963.

However, many larger signs were built as transportation routes expanded during the 1950s and 1960s. Huge billboards were erected along the major highways and rural roads and in urban centers. Billboards so cluttered the strips of land along the highways that they threatened to block views of the scenic landscapes. As a result, the federal Highway Beautification Act of 1965 was passed. The law was designed to remove unsightly billboards, but it did little to control the proliferation of signs.

In its present form, the act regulates the old billboards and requires cash payments to billboard owners who must tear down their signs. Policies of the Federal Highway Administration (FHWA) allowed billboard companies to destroy trees and shrubs on public land if the vegetation blocked the view of billboards. However, twenty-nine states prohibit such practices, and the FHWA changed its policy in 1990, probably due to environmental concerns and the Bush administration's goal of planting millions of trees. In addition, bills have been introduced in the U.S. Congress to ban billboards along federal highways and to stop the destruction of trees cut down only to provide a clear view of the signs.[9]

Most states regulate signs along state highways and most communities have some type of ordinance that restricts the size and location of outdoor advertising signs. But across the nation, a growing number of local government officials have expressed concern about visual pollution and the traffic hazards posed by billboards. Some officials would like to see stricter rules in regard to outdoor advertising. On the other hand, billboard owners and some local legislators fear that communities will lose revenues if billboard ads are restricted or banned.

While the very existence of billboards may be threatened in some communities, another type of outdoor advertising is becoming part of the urban scene: video monitors in subways, train terminals, and bus stations in major cities. These video systems present news and weather reports along with advertising beamed at travelers. Similar systems are being installed in malls to inform shoppers about a variety of topics and of course to advertise goods and services offered by mall retailers.

CHANGES IN PRINT AND BROADCAST MEDIA

With the advent of television about fifty years ago, communication experts and newscasters predicted that newspapers, magazines, and radio would become ineffective media for presenting advertising messages. Indeed, major advertisers today spend about half of their advertising dollars on TV commercials, and it is an increasingly powerful medium, reaching millions of people across the nation. But because TV advertising generally is much more expensive than ads placed in other media, TV commercials account for less than 22 percent of the total amount spent each year on advertising. Newspapers, on the other hand, receive more than 26 percent of the nation's advertising dollars annually, while magazines receive a little over 5 percent.[10]

Clearly, print ads still play a major role in carrying advertising messages to consumers. However, there have been changes over the years in how print media reach their audiences. Although the U.S. population has increased, the daily circulation of newspapers has remained about the same. Why? Some newspaper executives believe that illiteracy is one reason newspaper readership has remained static. At least 25 million Americans cannot read or write, and another 45 million to 47 million are functionally illiterate, or unable to read and write well enough to understand information in a newspaper (or to hold a job that requires literacy).[11]

In addition, surveys by major newspapers show that even among the reading population far fewer teenagers and young adults are reading newspapers than these groups did several generations ago. Many in these age groups report that they do not have time to read newspapers and instead learn about news events from TV newscasts and radio. Some get the information they need from newsletters, fax machines, and computer information services.

In order to attract more readers—and advertisers who want to reach those readers—some newspapers are trying new approaches. One is to send a digest-size newspaper by fax machine to subscribers. Another is to design more pages to appeal to young people, or to develop a newspaper that is more personalized, carrying practical information that people can use. Still others may attempt the kind of graphic format used by *USA Today*.

Nevertheless, journalists argue that the press was not established to entertain or to cater to people's wishes, conforming to what consumers and advertisers want. Professionals insist that newspapers should be free of influence and should exist in a free society to provide people with factual information about events that affect their lives, particularly in regard to government. That, as many national leaders through history have noted, is the reason the U.S. Constitution protects the freedom of the press. Abraham Lincoln put it simply: "Let the people know the facts and the country will be free."

Indeed, the free press provides Americans with a great deal of factual information. But since newspapers seldom are able to survive without the revenue from advertising, there is always the possibility that some advertisers will try to manipulate the news in their favor.[12]

Magazines, too, may be subject to advertiser influence. Most of the mass-circulation, or consumer, magazines depend on advertising to stay in business. Over the past decade, however, overall advertising in many of these magazines has been decreasing. In some instances, advertisers have switched from print ads to TV commercials.

To increase their income from advertising, some publications are developing advertising programs that tie in with books, videocassettes, and TV shows. For example, the Meredith Corporation, publishers of the well-known *Better Homes & Gardens Cookbook*, published a version of its cookbook for Kraft, complete with the familiar red-and-white checked cover. Then Meredith placed ads for the book in its magazines, including *Better Homes & Gardens* and *The Ladies' Home Journal.*[13]

Radio advertising also has been undergoing some changes. Since its earliest days in the 1920s, "U.S. broadcasting has been run as private enterprise with advertising as its primary source of funding," writes Bob Schulberg, marketing director for CBS Radio. Although advertisers today frequently prefer TV to radio as a medium for broadcasting their messages, they nevertheless still spend about $7.5 billion each year on radio commercials. As Schulberg notes, radio is the "ultimate personal medium"—in which programs are designed for particular audiences.

Thus, advertisers who sponsor such programs can direct their radio commercials to specific groups of listeners with similar interests. Like many other radio broadcasters, Schulberg believes that radio will be a potent advertising medium for many years to come, since it can reach people just about anywhere that a portable radio can be carried and tuned in.[14]

VIDEO TRENDS

Few people would argue about the staying power of television as a medium for advertising, but advertisers who use this medium continually search for innovative ways to reach consumers, to be noticed above the jumble of commercials. For example, a cable TV channel called Checkout Channel is being shown to shoppers standing in lines at some supermarket checkout counters. The shoppers are, in effect, captive audiences, because they do not want to leave the line until after they pay for the items they want. Thus, while they wait, they watch commercials along with the news and features on the TV channel.

Video devices also are being attached to the handles of supermarket shopping carts; the small screens list weekly specials or show ads for particular brands. In addition, some supermarket chains are installing electronic signs over aisles. The signs continually scroll a variety of advertising messages.

Another popular technique is the video news release, or VNR. VNRs are somewhat like printed news releases that are prepared by a company or organization and sent to newspapers and magazines. Obviously VNRs go to network and cable TV stations. They resemble news features: an announcer introduces the feature and experts tell the story, which is backed up by a variety of photographic and other visual materials.

Although there is no commercial as such, advertisers are able to promote their company names in a VNR by using pictures of a product or company logo or by having a company representative speak. Because the VNRs appear to be part of the news, viewers tend to believe that the information is unbiased reporting rather than a prepackaged story designed to present a company, organization, or product in a favorable light.

One more trendy technique is the "infomercial," which is a TV program that appears to be an information program or talk show. It may run thirty minutes or an hour and feature a celebrity who endorses a product. Some 2,000 of these programs are broadcast on independent or cable stations across the nation, and most of them inform viewers that they are watching a program-length commercial. But others try to avoid the appearance of advertising.

According to a report in *Money* magazine, the Federal Trade Commission (FTC), which regulates many kinds of marketing practices, has taken action against seven infomercials and the manufacturers of the products that were advertised. In one instance an Arizona company, Twin Star Productions, was required to "stop airing commercials for a male impotence 'remedy,' a baldness 'cure,' and a so-called diet patch—an adhesive disk attached to the skin that supposedly produces weight loss . . . [agreeing] to refund $1.5 million to dissatisfied viewers who bought the products."[15]

Whatever gimmicks advertisers use, there has been no slackening in the TV commercials designed to appeal to young people. As a result, many famous athletes, TV and movie stars appear in ads. While celebrity endorsements are common in commercials, never before have celebrities "hawked such expensive 'status' products," according to Consumers Union's report on advertisements aimed at young people.

The products advertised include athletic shoes, video games, jeans, and other costly goods that many families cannot realistically afford. Most of these products are advertised on music videos and cartoon shows that are favorites with children. The commercials create what Consumers Union calls "undue pressure on kids." As the report points out, "Recent news reports of kids beating, shooting, even killing other kids for their status fashions dramatically illustrate how powerful 'status sell' can be. . . . Of course, kids *can* stand up to the pressure from their peers and get along without costly products. . . . But it's not easy, nor is it fun. Kids shouldn't be put in that situation in the first place. . . . Celebrities have enormous potential to influence kids, yet that potential is pretty much directed by the corporate sector, which pays millions to have stars influence kids' brand preferences and loyalty."[16]

Consumers Union and other advocacy groups such as the Parent Teachers Association and Action for Children's Television have campaigned for years to restrict TV advertising aimed at young people. These groups say that many children's TV programs are in themselves no more than thirty-minute commercials and that some manufacturers design toys primarily to use them as a basis for TV shows in which the toys are the main characters.

In late 1990, the U.S. Congress passed the Children's Television Act, limiting the commercials on children's television programs to twelve minutes per hour on weekdays and ten and a half minutes per hour on weekends. In addition, the law requires the Federal Communications Commission (FCC) to determine whether stations are meeting children's educational needs, a condition required by a station's licensing agreement.

Another provision requires that the FCC determine whether or not toy-based shows are actually commercials rather than programs for kids. This could be the most controversial part of the law. Many educational shows such as "Sesame Street" have licensed manufacturers to produce toys based on the show, and the show could be considered a promotional effort to sell products.

Harold Shoup, executive vice president of the American Association of Advertising Agencies, argues that those who criticize TV advertising aimed at children have exaggerated the situation. He writes that "manufacturers of children's products closely follow guidelines established by the Council of Better Business Bureau's Children's Advertising Review Unit, which, since 1974, has had more than 270 commercials modified or discontinued." He contends as well that "free Saturday-morning TV programming—made possible by advertising support—is welcomed and valued by millions of parents as a highly acceptable diversion for children. And no one has yet proved that any amount of TV commercials harms children."[17]

Many advertisers and some economists say that more government regulation of TV commercials as well as of other types of ads are not necessary and could be harmful to the U.S. economy. Economic studies show that the prices of many products—from toys to gasoline—and a variety of services increase when advertising is restricted, but that prices decrease when regulations are lifted. One example frequently cited: attorneys once were prohibited from advertising their legal services but now can do so; as a result attorney fees have dropped in some communities and legal services are available to more people.

However, one legal expert, Professor O. Lee Reed of the University of Georgia at Athens, sees new regulations in the future for TV commercials, not only for children's shows but for others as well. Reed believes laws will limit "music, visual imagery, and 'slice-of-life' portrayals to sell products." He points out that advertisers claim that such legislation would violate first amendment rights to free speech. But the U.S. Supreme Court already had ruled against misleading advertising, and Reed believes dramatizations, graphics, and music could be construed as misleading. He predicts that advertisers will be required to limit advertising based on national appeals and instead present ads that inform consumers—that is, provide unadorned facts about goods and services.[18]

One type of advertising for which more stringent restrictions may be written is radio and TV commercials for alcoholic beverages. Several bills that include such restrictions have already been introduced in the U.S. Congress and would require that ads for alcoholic beverages carry messages warning users about the health hazards of the products. Some legislators want alcohol advertising on TV banned completely as tobacco advertising was in 1971, although tobacco companies still advertise heavily in other media. There are predictions that Congress will pass legislation banning tobacco advertising entirely as has been done in more than twenty other nations, including Canada and France.[19]

Would the American public like to see a total ban on cigarette advertising? That was what the Gallup organization wanted to find out in a telephone poll of 1,240 adults in July 1990. The survey showed respondents split on the issue, with 49 percent in favor of a complete ban and 48 percent opposed; the remaining 3 percent responded "don't know."[20]

CHAPTER SEVEN

SELLING CAUSES AND CANDIDATES

The fast-food company, McDonald's, teams up with the World Wildlife Federation, an environmental organization, to produce a booklet called *Wecology*, which explains what young people can do to protect the earth.

Another fast-food chain, Burger King, together with the shoe company Nike, develops a nationwide "Stay in School" campaign that stresses the importance of completing a high school education.

A coalition of businesses, foundations, and government agencies in Maryland launches a media blitz to call attention to its "Campaign for Our Children," a five-year program to stem adolescent pregnancies in the state, basically sending to girls between nine and fourteen years old the message "You don't need to have sex."

A marketing and public relations firm develops a public awareness program using a variety of media to inform people that clinical depression is a treatable disease, not just a temporary emotional problem of being "down in the dumps" or having "the blues."

Celebrities voluntarily give their time to appear in print

ads and TV and radio commercials supporting candidates for government offices or political causes such as gun control or animal protection.

Each of the efforts just described is a type of advertising or promotional campaign designed to shape or alter public opinion. Rather than selling consumer goods or services, the campaigns promote causes or candidates.

PUBLIC SERVICE ADVERTISING

Some of these promotional efforts are public service advertising or announcements called PSAs. The PSAs appear in print or broadcast media as *pro-bono* services, free or at reduced rates. (*Pro bono* is a shortened form of *pro bono publico*, a Latin term meaning "for the public good.")

Although PSAs probably have been in existence since the early days of the nation, an organized approach to this type of advertising began during World War II, when a voluntary association known as the War Advertising Council was formed. Members of the council prepared ads urging Americans to support the war effort. The ads helped persuade people to buy war bonds, to conserve metals and other scarce resources, to increase production in plants manufacturing equipment for the armed forces, and to take part in numerous volunteer programs, such as rolling bandages for the American Red Cross.

The association continued after the war, changing its name to the Advertising Council. Its members, who represent advertising agencies and the media, donate hundreds of millions of dollars in professional services each year for PSA campaigns coordinated by the council.

Advertising agencies and individuals provide pro bono services because they consider it a payback to the community in which their businesses operate. PSA campaigns also offer creative challenges, and if the campaigns are successful, they provide favorable publicity for the advertising agencies and other professionals involved in their creation.

Some PSA campaigns have been so effective that the symbols and slogans created have become an accepted part of American life. You are possibly familiar with Smokey the Bear, a character that came on the scene several decades ago. Smokey was introduced in an ad campaign designed to alert the public about fire prevention. The campaign's bottom-line message is still proclaimed widely across the land: "Only YOU can prevent forest fires."

Numerous other campaigns over the years have used advertising slogans and symbols to call attention to environmental problems ranging from the waste of natural resources to unsightly litter and toxic chemicals polluting the environment. PSAs also have helped inform the public about major health problems such as cancer, heart disease, and sexually transmitted diseases.

Advertising in the public interest has fostered better understanding of the need for nutritious foods and exercise to maintain good health. In addition, social problems have been addressed. Alcoholism, child abuse, racial discrimination, homelessness, the lack of adequate health care for the frail elderly, and the needs of the disabled for better access to public buildings, transportation and job opportunities are some examples of issues covered in PSA campaigns.

One of the largest PSA campaigns in recent years has been the combined effort of print and broadcast media nationwide to help stem the drug abuse problem. Since the mid-1980s, the media have provided time and space free of charge for antidrug messages. Articles and feature stories on drug abuse have been published consistently in newspapers and magazines, and TV specials on the problem have appeared on a regular basis. The campaign, along with antidrug educational programs conducted by volunteers in communities across the country, appears to be making a difference. According to a report in the *Washington Post*, several major studies show a steady decrease in drug use nationwide since 1985.[1]

Another major social and health problem, AIDS, is also

being addressed with PSA campaigns. A highly successful AIDS awareness campaign over a two-year period was initiated by the Oregon Health Division (OHD) during the latter part of the 1980s. Previous research had shown that there was a dire need in the state (and the nation as well) to correct a misconception that only homosexuals were at risk of being infected with the HIV virus that causes the acquired immune deficiency syndrome, or AIDS. Research showed that among those at risk were intravenous drug users and sexually active teens as well as people of color. There was also a need for public education about measures that would help prevent the spread of AIDS.

The Oregon Health Division selected Turtledove Clemens, an advertising and marketing agency in Portland, to create and develop materials for the campaign, the first aspect of which would be "to shock the general public out of their complacency about AIDS," said George Taylor, vice president, creative and production, at the agency, which provided its services on a pro bono basis.

"Our strategy was to get the word out to the general population that AIDS is a disease that can strike anyone who indulges in at-risk behavior. It was a complete mass-media PSA effort with donated time on TV and radio and donated space in newspapers (including high school papers). We developed strong visuals with daring headlines that stressed the need for protection, but because of our research, we knew that the media would not allow us to use the word 'condom' so we were careful to only include the word on materials such as posters targeted for groups who would not object," Taylor explained.

One poster that the agency developed came about because of a request from the gay community. It depicted a man in a bright yellow raincoat with the headline: "Good boys always wear their rubbers." The poster was so effective that many other groups have requested it because, as Taylor pointed out, "people just think it's a great poster of a great-looking guy. The demand for it now far exceeds supply." In fact, many of the materials developed for the Oregon AIDS campaign have received national and international advertising awards and have been syndicated to other health and governmental organizations all across the United States and in Canada.

The strategy for the next part of the campaign was to target specific groups. "Part of the process involved extensive research, including fourteen input sessions with community-based groups, health officials, law enforcement, and even prison inmates," Taylor said. "We sought to unite people all over the state to fight AIDS together, so we used the theme People United Against AIDS."[2]

Volunteer groups, community leaders, and government officials conducted educational programs, using media materials developed by the advertising agency. The total campaign has been so successful that calls to the state's AIDS hot-line number (included on the Oregon materials) have increased dramatically.

SELLING CAUSES WITH PAID ADS AND PROMOTIONS

Some nonprofit groups pay for advertising or fund-raising campaigns (as opposed to using PSAs), formulating their own promotional materials or working with advertising agencies or public relations firms that specialize in promoting social or environmental causes. Most nonprofit groups solicit funds and promote their causes through direct mail. It is a medium that fund-raisers believe is vital for communicating messages that may not be used in broadcast and print media, particularly if the messages criticize advertisers or express political views different from those of the major media.

"Nearly every means of producing and efficiently distributing information in the United States is monopolized for commercial purposes," writes Herb Chao Gunther, executive director of the Public Media Center. "There just aren't many effective ways of reaching like-minded people and organizing them into constituencies ready to fight for the causes we care about. Direct mail has proven to be one of the best and most affordable activists tools we have."[3]

Yet direct-mail solicitations, if successful, usually result in a response of only 2 percent. So when non-profit groups want to promote their causes or to communicate messages quickly, they usually design advertising campaigns for TV networks along with promotional materials placed in other media. But because TV stations can place PSAs wherever they have an available time slot, which could be just before signoff or some other period when there are few viewers, the advertising might have little impact. However, if non-profit groups pay for TV time, they have more control over when their promotional material will be aired and what their messages will say.

One organization, the Natural Resources Defense Council (NRDC), a research and law firm working to protect the environment, decided in 1989 to develop a paid advertising campaign to call attention to synthetic chemical residues on foods. Previously, the group had tried many tactics to persuade the federal government to ban the use of dangerous pesticides, but little or no action was taken. Then NRDC analyzed data on Alar, the trade name given for a chemical used to enhance the growth of applies, which produces a substance known as UDMH that causes cancer in laboratory animals. NRDC's analysis showed that Alar residues on apples increased the cancer risk for young children.

Rather than simply announce the findings in a new release or through other print media, NRDC paid two public relations firms to help them get the story aired on the popular TV shows "60 minutes" and "Donahue." The group also created a TV commercial in which actress Meryl Streep explained to a youngster why fresh fruits and vegetables had to be washed to remove toxic chemicals sprayed on them.

The campaign brought more results within a few weeks

than was possible over several years of lawsuits and continued pressure on federal legislators. Consumers refused to buy apples or products made with apples treated with Alar. Some food processors also refused to use Alar-treated apples, and supermarket chains across the United States announced that they not only would refuse to sell Alar-treated apples but also would test other produce for pesticide residues and post the results for customers. Eventually, the manufacturer of Alar stopped selling the product.[4]

Some food scientists, biochemists, and others have criticized NRDC's promotional campaign, calling it misleading since, they argue, the NRDC report was flawed. One critic, Joseph D. Rosen, a Rutgers food science professor who researches food toxicology, states that the risk assessments used by NRDC were based on "worst-case scenarios, not actual risk." In an article for *Issues in Science and Technology*, Rosen claims (as have other critics) that NRDC ignored studies conducted by an independent Scientific Advisory Panel, which said that animal tests to determine the effects of Alar were not a valid basis for banning the chemical.[5]

Yet members of the U.S. Congress criticized the Scientific Advisory Panel, because seven out of eight of the scientists on the panel were consultants for the chemical industry at the time they determined that Alar did not pose a high risk and should not be banned. None of the scientists were public health experts or pediatricians who might have expertise on the effects of chemicals on children. As sociologist and science writer Joan Goldstein noted, scientists do not work in a vacuum.

Their professional opinions are shaped by their discipline and the organizations for which they work. Public health experts may view the evidence from a totally different perspective than the toxicologist, for example. Public health experts may ask what is the health effect upon people, and search for statistical evidence to back themselves up. Toxicologists may focus on chemical properties tested in the laboratory, and their work is often very valuable to industry.[6]

CARING COMPANIES?

In recent years, a growing number of advertising campaigns for nonprofit groups have been supported by business firms whose company names appear in the ads promoting causes. Or the promotions for nonprofit groups are linked in some way with the sponsoring company. Many companies that support promotional campaigns for nonprofit groups or causes do so because they are committed to the well-being of the public. They also want to establish positive images in the minds of viewers, listeners, or readers. After all, a business is part of the community, and community welfare can have an effect on the business and vice versa.

But promotional campaigns that appear to benefit the public while at the same time promoting a product or service can backfire at times. In one campaign, Quaker Oats agreed to pay for a series of TV spots on health issues developed by the American Medical Association (AMA). Actor Wilford Brimley, who has appeared in many Quaker Oats ads and has been closely tied with the company's oatmeal products, presented the AMA announcements. By linking the health information with Brimley, the medical association appeared to be endorsing Quaker Oats products. Since the medical profession is supposed to be free of commercial influence, some TV stations refused to air the ads.[7]

Promotional campaigns also come about because companies want to offset adverse publicity or negative public images. Oil companies, for example, are trying to counter negative perceptions about their activities. The Exxon Corporation is one company that has been battered with bad publicity, primarily due to an incident in 1989 when its tanker the *Exxon Valdez* ran aground in Alaska's Prince William Sound, spilling nearly 11 million gallons of oil.

The Exxon oil spill and other spills over the years have caused great environmental damage, polluting seas and shores and killing aquatic life, birds, and plants. In addition, oil and gasoline, when burned, produce chemical compounds that contaminate the air; some are highly toxic, others are responsible for smog or are precursors of acid rain.

How are oil companies trying to change their images? Some have developed advertising campaigns that focus on reformulated gasoline. In reformulating gasoline, refineries reduce some components that help produce smog and add MTBE (methyl tertiary butyl ether), which raises the oxygen levels of the gas and allows it to burn cleaner. (The formula for making a cleaner gasoline has been around for some time, and environmentalists and many consumers wonder why improvements were not made years ago. The federal Clean Air Act Amendments of 1990 now require that reformulated gasoline be sold in the nine cities with the highest levels of smog, with Los Angeles at the top of the list.)

Other efforts by the oil industry to show environmental responsibility include promotion for the Marine Spill Response Corporation. The industry established five response centers at varied locations so that, should a spill occur, they would be prepared to act immediately, which could prevent environmental damage. Petroleum companies also say they are spending millions of dollars each year on environmental projects such as waste cleanup.

GETTING ON THE "GREEN" BANDWAGON

Oil companies certainly are not the only firms looking for a place on the "green," or environmental, bandwagon. Does that mean that companies are genuinely interested in environmental issues? In some cases, yes, according to a report in a special environmental issue of *Advertising Age*. Dozens of national and multinational firms have developed in-house recycling programs as well as encourage consumer recycling programs. Some companies are using more recycled materials in their products, cutting back on the amount of packaging they use, reducing waste, and making goods more durable and repairable. In addition, there are efforts by firms to produce goods and services that do not harm the environment.[8]

Why this "green revolution," as it has come to be called? Over the past decade or more, surveys of consumers have shown a consistent increase in the number of people who say that their purchasing decisions frequently are determined by environmental concerns. In one survey of 313 women shopping in a mall, 82 percent of the respondents said they had changed purchasing habits because of environmental concerns; 56 percent refused to buy a product that would harm the environment; 77 percent said a company's environmental reputation influenced their choice of brands.[9]

Poll takers and public-opinion researchers also have found that more and more consumers believe their health is at risk because of environmental degradation and are demanding goods and services that are not hazards. As a result, companies are scrambling to try to show that they and their products are environmentally safe. Consider a few examples:

- Phillips Petroleum advertises its support of the Avian Research Center that is attempting to preserve the endangered bald eagle, the nation's symbol, by raising eaglets and releasing them into their natural habitats.

- Amway sponsors ads that appear to be articles about people who are taking action to clean up pollution or enhance the environment in other ways.

- Minute Maid In-The-Box ads say the company will plant a tree "in your name" at a national park; the consumer pays seventy-five cents for the tree and the company matches the amount.

- Sears advertises outdoor clothing from Oshkosh B'Gosh, saying that the two companies are donating funds to The Nature Conservancy in order to "preserve our nation's natural environment" and ensure that people have a place to wear the clothing that Sears sells.

But *D&B Reports*, a business magazine, cautions companies to "beware of trying to position a product as environmentally friendly when it really isn't." Many people, particularly those who have educated themselves on "green consuming," are on the alert for products that do not live up to their advertising claims. The result may be consumer distrust and a boycott of products.[10]

One environmental group, the Environmental Defense Fund, called for a boycott when ads appeared touting garbage bags by Hefty and GLAD that supposedly were "photodegradable" (able to break down in sunlight). As environmentalists are quick to point out, plastic is not truly photodegradable or even biodegradable. Some plastic can break down in sunlight or in composting piles that allow air and water to circulate through them, but most disposable plastic materials end up in landfills that are tightly compacted. Not only plastic but all kinds of materials can remain entombed and intact for decades since air, water, and sunlight, cannot do their part to decompose materials. Thus, advertising claims by the companies producing the plastic products were misleading and the Environmental Defense Fund suggested: "Don't get GLAD; get mad." After such protests, and also lawsuits, the ads were retracted.

Companies that manufacture disposable diapers also have been forced to revise their advertising, since these products are dumped in landfills, too, and may have a longer life than the babies who wore them. In 1991, Procter & Gamble, which manufactures disposable diapers along with many other products, began testing a new disposable diaper that the company says will biodegrade and become compost that can be used as fertilizer. In addition, the company is granting funds to cities that build municipal composting plants, which can convert solid waste into fertilizer within two weeks. To encourage support for composting, the company has placed ads in a number of consumer magazines. Using the headline "This baby is growing up in disposable diapers," the ads show a tree planted in soil enriched with composting material.[11]

How do consumers distinguish between what is environmentally benign and what is harmful? "It's not easy being green," as many consumers who have tried to buy "ecologically correct" products would tell you. But perhaps there is help for consumers who want more than hype or advertising pitches about environmentally safe products.

Several groups in the United States have set up programs to identify products that do not harm the environment, following in the footsteps of Germany's environmental agency. The German agency was one of the first worldwide to use a logo—the Blue Angel seal—to label environmentally safe products in several categories.

In 1990, the nonprofit Alliance for Social Responsibility in New York City launched a Green Seal program, developing specifications for its seal, which will be placed on "earth-safe" products sold in the United States. Another nonprofit organization, the Green Cross Certification Company, has developed an "environmental seal of approval," which it awards to companies and products that meet such environmental standards as energy efficiency and use of recycled materials. Several major discount store chains, such as Wal-Mart and K mart, are selling a line of products that carry a "green" sticker or label.

There are a number of published guides for "buying green." A popular one is *Shopping for a Better World* by the Council on Economic Priorities. It lists information about company practices that affect the environment (as well as other social issues). Many nationally distributed magazines and newspapers also have carried articles about being a green consumer. Some examples: A supermarket shopper's guide with information about the environmental impact of some products appeared in the February 1990 issue of *Changing Times*. And the May-June 1990 issue of *Greenpeace* carried a feature called "A Bill of Goods? Green Consuming In Perspective."

In another arena, a legal task force with representatives from eleven states is attempting to set standards that manufacturers can follow in regard to claims about the environment. Minnesota Attorney General Hubert H. Humphrey III, spokesman for the group, has pointed out that "we are knee-deep in environmental hype. Manufacturers, marketers and regulators should work together to set standards for claims for truly green products."[12]

Working toward that goal, the task force has recommended "that the federal government adopt a national regulatory scheme establishing definitions for environmental marketing claims to be used in the labeling, packaging and promotion of products on the basis of environmental attributes." However, states do not want the federal government to pre-empt regulations they have established; California, New York, and others already have enacted laws that govern the use of environmental terms such as "recyclable" and "biodegradable." But the task force has recommended that the federal government develop uniform definitions for green marketing terms. In addition, the group would like environmental claims on products to be as specific as possible and supported by reliable scientific evidence.[13]

POLITICAL ADS

Political advertising is somewhat akin to cause advertising, incorporating some of the same promotional techniques. But ads for political candidates are in a class of their own. In the first place, most advertising dollars in a campaign for major political offices are spent on TV commercials, which are not regulated by any laws or review boards and cannot be censored by broadcasters. Political ads are protected as free speech by the First Amendment to the U.S. Constitution and in many instances, free speech allows candidates to make charges against opponents that may be half-truths or even false.

Since TV commercials are expensive, most political ads are only 30-second spots, allowing little time for detail. Frequently the ads are nasty—"quick-hit attack commercials" as newspaper columnist David Broder called them. Before the 1990 congressional elections, Broder, in his syndicated column that appears in newspapers across the nation, warned readers that he was going to be "a crank" about the way such commercials degraded political campaigns. He called for journalists to point out the "exaggerations, distortions and plain lies such ads often contain."[14]

Some newspapers and magazines did publish articles that critiqued political ads, explaining clearly what was true and false in them. Several TV commentators followed suit. And the public approved of the practice, according to a national survey conducted for *Time* and the Cable News Network. Of the one thousand adults polled, 66 percent said they would favor more media reports on misleading information contained in ads for political candidates. A large majority of survey respondents—85 percent—said they thought political advertising has been getting worse in the last few elections.[15]

Political ads not only charge a candidate's opponent with misdeeds; they also are used to create an overall negative impression of an opponent (in contrast to the candidate who is presented in a positive light). Special effects frequently are used in TV commercials to enhance the image of a candidate. A candidate may speak to a group, which can be made to appear larger and more animated than it actually is by the way the camera focuses on the scene and by adding a sound track with applause and cheers.

Makeup also can help improve the appearance of a candidate, covering up wrinkles or a shiny nose or other feature that might be distracting to viewers. In addition, TV film can be edited to show the candidate more favorably than the opponent, simply by contrasting a pleasing view of the candidate with the worst possible view of the opponent.

There are many other camera tricks as well as many other forms of political advertising and promotion that can be used to amplify a candidate's image. Perhaps a candidate will appear at an event that she or he knows will be a "photo opportunity"—one at which news photographers will be present—so the candidate can be assured that her or his photo will appear on TV news and in newspapers.

Because so much political advertising is misleading and frequently designed to sling mud at opponents, critics of political ads have been calling for reforms in the process. As advertising critic Bob Garfield put it: "Every campaign ad should bear a disclaimer . . . WARNING: POLITICAL ADVERTISING CAN LEGALLY DISTORT THE TRUTH."[16]

Some would like to see a voluntary review board established, similar to the panel that reviews product ads to determine whether they are deceptive. Others would like federal legislation passed to regulate political ads, although it is likely that such regulations would be challenged as an infringement on free speech.

Another proposal for reform calls for TV stations to allow time for candidates who have been attacked to respond to charges. One more proposition is for TV networks to allow candidates to appear on broadcasts free of charge but only to discuss public issues and their approaches to governing.

If political advertising does not provide more factual information about candidates and their views, many campaign consultants believe that ever larger numbers of citizens simply will not vote. As it is, the number of eligible voters who participate in a presidential election has dropped consistently since 1960. Voter turnout in the United States is now the lowest of any nation with a democratic form of government. Although there are many reasons why people do not exercise their right to vote, the fact remains that political advertising does little to inform the voters and sometimes is so disgusting that it turns people against politicians and politics in general.

Yet citizens who want to vote intelligently do have a choice. They can find other sources besides television for information about candidates, such as in-depth newspaper and magazine articles. In some cases, particularly local elections, voters can interview candidates, questioning them on a variety of topics. And voters can protest distortions or lies in political ads just as they protest misleading or fraudulent ads for goods and services.

CHAPTER EIGHT

ON GUARD

Most of us know that it is the rare advertisement that presents literal, unadorned facts about a product or service. After all, if you were trying to sell your car, you would not write an ad that describes the car's flaws. Instead you would provide facts about the features of your car that would persuade someone to buy it. In a similar vein, if you were applying for a job, you would not try to sell an employer on your shortcomings. Instead you would present factual information about your work skills to show that you qualify for a job.

Most producers of goods and services are attempting to do the same thing—advertise what they have to sell in an informative and appealing way. But sometimes advertising messages are distorted by words and images that have little to do with factual information.

How do you distinguish between facts and exaggeration in the advertising messages? One way is to be on guard for tricks and gimmicks used in advertising, and also to be alert for the small number of people who deliberately use deceptive advertising practices to cheat and defraud.

TRICK WORDS

Words in advertising messages sometimes are used in tricky ways—that is, they may appear to provide information about a product or service but in reality are statements open to many interpretations. Consider some common modifying words used in advertising such as "wonderful," "best," "true," "fast," "exciting," "virtually," "beautiful," and "glamorous." These are tricky terms because they are abstract modifiers; what is beautiful to one person may be ugly to another. Using such words is not considered deceptive because most people understand that they are used in hyperbole, a kind of hype or overstatement. But when advertisers make specific claims for what their products will do, and the claims are challenged by consumers, the advertiser may be legally charged with fraud, an offense that can result in fines and/or prison sentences.

One way that advertisers are able to avoid making false statements is to use doublespeak, or language that appears to say something but instead is mere jargon or deliberate gobbledygook used to circumvent facts. Doublespeak can be used to overwhelm people with words, to make ordinary events seem extraordinary, or to make statements that seem authoritative or factual but on analysis are meaningless.

William Lutz explains in his book on the subject how people in many walks of life use doublespeak to distort the truth, and he includes many examples of doublespeak in advertising. He points out that ads frequently include the helping word "helps" with a strong verb—"helps stop," "helps relieve," "helps cure," "helps fight"—a tricky way to avoid making a claim. Lutz writes:

A toothpaste ad says, "Helps prevent cavities," but it doesn't say it will actually prevent cavities. Brushing your teeth regularly, avoiding sugars in food, and flossing daily will also help prevent cavities. A liquid cleaner ad says, "Helps keep your home germ free," but it doesn't say it actually kills germs, nor does it even specify which germs it might kill.[1]

You can probably make up your own list of gobbledygook phrases: doublespeak advertising that appears to be making important, authentic claims about what products or services will do, but really says very little. If you take time to analyze the language of advertising, you can sort out the tricky words and phrases.

Ask yourself, for example, what does "new and improved" mean? What is new about the product, how is it improved? If an advertisement says, "when you want the very best," do you immediately ask "the very best of what?" And if you filled in the "what," then how do you know you really want it?

Processed food ads frequently include a statement such as "½ the calories" but do you know how many calories there were to begin with and what the product is being compared to? Maybe you buy a soft drink because it is advertised as having "the right taste." How can a taste be "right" or "wrong"? Even if right is used to mean "appropriate" or "suitable," what is "suitable taste" and how do you define your taste anyway?

If you see an ad for antidandruff shampoo, do you associate "anti—" with "against" and wonder whether just being against something will help eliminate the dandruff problem? Does the cold medicine you buy "work fast?" How do you know? Can you compare it with another brand? How do you measure "fast"? In seconds, minutes, or what?

Whatever the advertising messages, the point is to check out the way words are used. As Lutz puts it, "Remember, the ad is trying to get you to buy a product, so it will put the product in the best possible light, using any device, trick, or means legally allowed."[2]

PHONY MARKDOWNS

You have seen the signs on store windows: "50 percent off!" "Prices slashed in half!" "Huge discounts!" These are another form of doublespeak advertising, because you do not know from the signs what goods are being discounted or how much the goods or services cost before they were marked down.

Certainly many discounts are legitimate. Merchants mark down the prices of goods and services in order to sell them. If store owners have large stocks of goods, their cash is tied up in the merchandise and cannot be used to pay utility costs, payroll, and other expenses. Discounting merchandise is a way to generate income and can offer real bargains to consumers.

But some major stores have misled consumers with big discount sales. In some states, consumer protection agencies are prosecuting retail stores that use discounts as part of an advertising scheme to attract customers.

How does the scheme work? First, the prices of goods are inflated—marked *up*—from the original or usual prices. Retailers inflate the prices two weeks or so before a planned sale, then cut the prices to a more reasonable level, and then reduce prices again so that the large discounts can be advertised.

In California, the Los Angeles district attorney brought charges against two large department stores, Nordstrom and May Company, for falsely advertising discounts of up to 60 percent for merchandise, when in fact the true discount was only 10 percent. According to the *Los Angeles Times*, the companies paid fines of $200,000 and $295,000 respectively for their markdown practices, although neither store admitted that its advertisements were misleading.[3]

FINE PRINT

Perhaps you have heard the warning to "Read the fine print!" on a label, advertisement, guarantee, or consumer agreement. It is a precaution that should be heeded, since information in small type may limit how you can use a product, or spell out conditions that are not described elsewhere.

Many small-print statements are used to modify the meanings of claims in an ad. Perhaps you see an offer for a "cash refund*" on a product and find out from the disclaimer in tiny type following the asterisk that your refund is only good on your next purchase. Automobile ads are notorious for their fine-print messages. Vehicles may be offered at a special discount price, but qualifying statements indicate that only a limited number of models are for sale at the special price. Lifetime warranties may be advertised for products ranging from bikes to cameras to video recorders. But watch out for the fine print that might list dozens of restrictions on a warranty.

Consumer Reports and the *AARP Bulletin* (a newsletter for members of the American Association of Retired Persons) warned readers about the fine print used in a 1990 fund-raising campaign conducted by the Republican Campaign Committee. In a clever turnabout, the committee mailed out hundreds of thousands of "gift" checks for $25 to possible donors.

But there was a catch. An agreement in small type was printed on the back of the check. Anyone who endorsed the check also signed the agreement, which "authorized the committee to make electronic withdrawals from the person's bank account at the rate of $12.50 a month, meaning the committee would have its $25 back in two months," AARP reports. "But after two months, which the committee call[ed] a trial period, it could keep billing the person $12.50" for the rest of that person's life. Letters sent along with the "gift" checks did explain how the endorsements worked and also that a person could cancel the arrangement by calling his or her bank. But after several states sued to prohibit the mailings, the campaign was stopped.[4]

SCAMS, SWINDLES, AND HOAXES

Although most companies offer legitimate goods and services, and most nonprofit organizations solicit funds for worthwhile causes, there are still those who intentionally defraud. A con artist employs many of the same types of advertising and promotional methods as a legitimate business person, so it sometimes is very difficult to tell the difference between a swindle and an honest business practice.

Swindlers frequently take advantage of people when they are most vulnerable, such as during the Christmas season when many people are feeling charitable and are in a giving spirit. This is a time when many phony charity workers solicit funds by mail, phone, or door-to-door appeals. Their "causes" may appear legitimate because they use familiar terms to request funds for "the homeless," "the disabled," or "the poor." But the donations do not go to any social service organization. Instead, the crooks keep what they collect.

Perhaps the best defense against fake fund-raisers is to ask plenty of questions. Request identification from them and ask about their purported organizations. If you have doubts, tell the solicitor you are going to check out the information with the police or other authority.

Fraudulent home-improvement schemes also can be seasonal, occurring most frequently in the spring and summer. Con artists might convince homeowners that they need to fix a chimney, replace a furnace, put siding on a home, blacktop a driveway, install new windows, or exterminate termites.

Before accepting the word of a stranger who claims to be a home-improvement expert, homeowners can check with well-established local repair people for advice. Then before turning over any money or signing any contract, a homeowner can check with the local Better Business Bureau to see if there have been reports about swindlers in the area.

A variation of the home-improvement scheme has been used to try to bilk small businesses of advertising dollars. A person who purports to be a representative for a publishing company goes to one small business after another in a community, soliciting payment for ads that already appear in the publication. Usually the publication contains statistics and information on a topic like crime or drug abuse, but it is primarily full of advertising. The problem is that business owners or employees have not authorized publication of the ads. But some business owners are led to believe that they forgot about placing the ads or that their employees authorized placement, so they are prodded into making payments. Even if a business person authorizes placement of an ad, the publication in which it appears may not be distributed widely, if it is distributed at all.

To guard against such schemes, the Better Business Bureau advises business people to ask to see a bulk mailing receipt or other evidence that more than a few copies of the publication have been produced. In addition, the bureau and state consumer protection offices tell business owners that they are under no obligation to pay for unauthorized ads.

One of the most persistent scams is the chain letter that appears to promote some kind of home business or a way to earn money at home. If you receive such a letter, you will probably be asked to send a dollar (or much larger sum) to the first person on the list at the end of the letter. You would be instructed to remove that person's name from the list and add your name to the bottom. You would then be asked to make copies of the letter and to send one each to ten or twenty other people. In time, you are told, your name will reach the top of the list, and you are promised thousands of dollars from the many individuals who supposedly will respond.

Although chain letters usually claim to be legal, they are not. The only people who make money on chain letters are those who start them or are in on the beginning of this scheme. After all, by the time one person sends out twenty letters, and those twenty people send out twenty more, there are already four hundred letters out. Multiply again by twenty and the total is 8,000. A little more arithmetic and common sense will tell you that the chain will be broken before thousands receive their letters.

Within the past few years, another deceptive practice has emerged. An increasing number of consumers have been victims of misleading or fraudulent promotions by companies that entice people to call 900 numbers. Certainly 900 numbers are legitimate marketing tools for many advertisers, and the service has been growing rapidly over the past decade, generating over $1 billion a year. But those that abuse the service may promote phony contests or offer information, which usually is provided by a recorded voice giving general facts about a product or information that is common knowledge and ends up being worthless to the caller.

One common scam using the 900 service is an offer of a luxury "gift." Perhaps you get a card or letter in the mail or a computer-generated telephone call telling you that you have won airplane tickets to a resort area or an automobile or some other major prize. All you have to do to collect your bounty is call a 900 number (for which you are charged) and pay for delivery and other expenses. Usually, you must give a credit card number in order to charge the expenses—no check or money order or cash accepted. If you fall for the scam, you will receive no prize, but the credit card number you revealed may be used for many unauthorized purchases.

In some cases, callers have responded to promotions for contests or for "talk lines, calling 900 numbers to answer a quiz or to rap or give an opinion on such topics as whether Elvis is alive or dead. When young children call, they may not realize that there is a charge (several dollars per minute plus the fee for the marketing service) or that the costs for a call can mount quickly. There have been news reports from across the country of youngsters who have run up telephone bills of thousands of dollars. Adult callers, too, have unwittingly accrued hefty phone charges.

During 1990 and 1991, so many consumers made complaints about being misled or duped by 900-number services that some state legislatures passed laws regulating these services. And in September 1991, the Federal Communications Commission issued new rules to control the use of 900 numbers. Providers charging more than $2.00 per call must deliver a message informing callers of the price and describing the service or product being offered, allowing time for a caller to hang up without being charged.

In addition, when children are urged to call a 900 number, the provider must issue a warning about the cost and nature of the call. FCC rulings also make it illegal to provide a service whereby a child can hold a phone near the television set and tones produced from a program automatically dial the 900 number.

Before the FCC rulings went into effect, some companies already had made it a practice to waive charges if 900-number calls made by children were unauthorized. They also have provided a service that allows customers to block calls to 900 numbers—no one can access the number without authorization.

CORPORATE DECEPTIONS

Most national and international companies expend a great deal of effort in trying to gain and maintain the trust of consumers, but some hoaxes have tarnished the reputations of well-known firms. An example is the Beech-Nut Nutrition Corporation. For several years, company executives were able to defraud consumers and outsmart federal and state government officials. As Consumers Union explained:

> For more than 50 years, parents depended on Beech-Nut Nutrition Corp. to provide nutritious, natural, healthful, food for their babies. They trusted Beech-Nut's reputation for quality. They believed Beech-Nut's promise to use only natural ingredients—no artificial flavorings, no preservatives, no colorings—promises made repeatedly in ads . . .
>
> Then Beech-Nut breached that trust. From 1977 to 1983, the product Beech-Nut sold as "100% fruit juice, no sugar added" contained little or no apple juice. It was an apple-flavored concoction that one company chemist later described as "a fraudulent chemical cocktail."[5]

Although there were a number of investigations into the operations of the company, Beech-Nut officials were able to avoid prosecution. In one instance, after New York State authorities tested Beech-Nut's imitation juice and found that it was not what the company claimed it to be, Beech-Nut shipped all of the product out of the country.

The company also was able to stall Food and Drug Administration (FDA) investigators who had no authority to obtain the company's records or to force people to testify against the firm. FDA investigators had to refer their findings to the U.S. Justice Department for prosecution. It took state and federal governments at least ten years to prosecute the company; during that time the company was able to continue to sell its products, collecting at least $60 million for flavored water labeled apple juice. Finally, in 1988, Beech-Nut's president, Neils Hoyvald, and vice-president of operations John Lavery were convicted of conspiracy, mail fraud, and other violations. Each was fined $100,000 and sentenced to a one-year prison term. The company was fined $2 million for violating FDA regulations.

Consumers Union tested Beech-Nut products after that time and "found no evidence of adulteration in the products," but pointed out that conditions exist for a repeat of a similar type of fraud. The consumer organization believes that the FDA needs stronger regulatory powers in order to prevent deception in the food and drug industries.[6]

However, the FDA has uncovered other fraudulent practices that have been prosecuted. For example, action was taken against Tulkoff's Horseradish Company, which according to the FDA

was substituting potatoes for horseradish in its products. Although company officials went to great lengths to cover up the practice, FDA investigators found at the firm large quantities of hidden potatoes, some of which were kept in a secret compartment. . . . Both the company and two responsible individuals pleaded guilty to adulterating charges and were fined a total of $11,500.[7]

Another fraud case focused on two multimillion dollar companies called Overeaters, Inc. and Health Care Products, Inc. Both companies are in the Tampa, Florida, area and advertise and distribute their weight-loss products—Bodi-Trim, Dietol-7, and Cal-Ban 3000—nationwide. The companies falsely claimed in their advertising that consumers who used their products could "Eat all you want and still lose weight with no exercise or calorie restrictions." However, researchers found that the companies' products did not bring about weight loss as advertised and in many instances were harmful. According to a United Press International report, many users developed rashes and intestinal problems.[8]

Volvo Cars of North America, a subsidiary of the Swedish company AB Volvo, was another company charged in

1990 with deceptive advertising. TV commercials filmed in Austin, Texas, showed a Volvo station wagon being run over by a "monster truck" (a giant pickup). In the film the Volvo was able to withstand the crunch while competing makes of cars were smashed. Questions and complaints about the commercial were sent to the popular consumer advocate David Horowitz and his show called "Fight Back!," which is shown on fifty-five TV stations and was partly responsible for an investigation by the Texas attorney general.

The investigation revealed that the Volvos used in the film had been reinforced with steel and wooden bars and competing makes of cars were weakened by removing supports. Horowitz noted that "the irony about Volvo is that it's one of the safest cars made," and previous investigations into the company's ads had shown that Volvos lived up to their safety claims.

The advertising agency, which was responsible for the commercial and had represented Volvo for twenty-three years, resigned the account. Volvo ran ads in Texas newspapers as well as in *USA Today* and the *Wall Street Journal* to explain why the commercials were withdrawn. In addition, Volvo reimbursed the Texas attorney general's office for the legal fees and other costs of the investigation.

A coalition of consumer and health groups labeled Volvo's ad "a classic fraud" when presenting its annual "Hall of Shame" awards at the end of 1990. But apparently sales have not been hurt, and many consumers blame the ad agency, not the company, for the misleading commercials.[9]

CHAPTER NINE

CONSUMER ACTION AND PROTECTION

Although many federal and state laws today are designed to protect consumers from fraudulent or misleading advertising and swindlers in the marketplace, most of these laws came about only within recent decades. Until the 1960s, most laws governing goods and services offered for sale in the United States and England were based on the legal doctrine of *caveat emptor*, Latin for "let the buyer beware."

If you were buying a horse, pair of boots, or other merchandise, you would be expected to examine them to find out if they were defective. Vendors, on the other hand, were expected to exaggerate the qualities of whatever livestock or merchandise they offered for sale; buyers were expected to understand that overstatements were common practice. Thus, courts would not hold advertisers legally responsible for the claims they made about their products or services.

This doctrine served as the basis for marketplace transactions for centuries. However, people did not automatically cheat each other. After all, most people lived in small rural communities or closely knit neighborhoods in cities and depended on each other for goods and services. If a wagon maker sold a defective wagon to a farmer, the farmer might turn around and sell a moldy bag of grain to the wagon maker. So it made sense to follow the Golden Rule and to trust one another.[1]

BEGINNINGS OF CONSUMER PROTECTION

Some of the first consumer-protection laws in the United States were passed during the late 1800s and early 1900s. It was a time when huge companies monopolized some industries and controlled prices, and some, such as the meat-packing industry, endangered public health. Not only were conditions in some meat-packing plants filthy, but meat packers also slaughtered sick animals along with healthy ones, passing the meat on to markets for human consumption.

The Sherman Antitrust Act enacted in 1890 banned business monopolies that destroyed free and fair competition and gouged consumers. Later, the federal Pure Food and Drug Act was passed and the Food and Drug Administration was established. In 1938, the federal Food, Drug, and Cosmetic Act set standards to regulate the safety of these products. Still, devious business people could side-step laws because they were not enforced consistently over the years.

In the twentieth century, one of the catalysts for consumer protection was a book published in 1927 called *Your Money's Worth*. Written by Stuart Chase, an economist, and Frederick J. Schlink, an engineer in White Plains, New York, the book explained how products could be tested to determine whether they lived up to their claims. The book became a best-seller and prompted Schlink to set up a small testing operation in his garage. He called it Consumers' Research.

A few years later, Schlink and Arthur Kallet collaborated on another book titled *100 Million Guinea Pigs*. Published in 1933, the book described how Americans were "unwitting test animals in a gigantic experiment with poisons conducted by food, drug, and cosmetic manufacturers." This book, too, became a best-seller, and played a major part in the establishment of Consumers' Research as a national, nonprofit consumer protection organization that has been operating ever since.[2]

Basically the two books and Consumers' Research (CR) called attention to the fact that consumers did not have enough information to evaluate products or advertising for products. Thus, consumers could not make wise buying decisions, and shoddy products remained in the marketplace. Consumers' Research pioneered consumer product testing, publishing its evaluations for the general public and for educational groups. Its monthly magazine, *Consumers' Research*, now runs articles focusing on consumer issues, covering such topics as banking, auto safety, pesticides, and health care.[3]

CR's basic approach in regard to consumer protection is to provide factual information about goods and services so that consumers can decide for themselves how to spend their money. Many of the opinion articles in the magazine emphasize that goods and services should be produced and sold in a "free market" (with as little government regulation as possible), since restrictions frequently increase the costs of goods and services.

Not long after Consumers' Research was established, some workers within the organization formed a union, which led to disagreements with management and eventually a bitter strike. As a result, thirty or so workers left Consumers' Research and in 1936 established another nonprofit group, Consumers Union of United States (CU). The group helps to inform consumers by testing a variety of products, comparing them with others of the same type. CU also rates products and services according to quality and price, which helps consumers in their buying decisions. Such information is published in *Consumer Reports* and, where appropriate, also in *Zillions* for kids. No advertising is accepted by either magazine.

CU also reports on new laws affecting consumers and brings dishonest marketing and advertising practices to the attention of the public. In addition, CU has conducted a number of studies on consumer affairs, such as *Selling America's Kids*, and has produced TV specials, educational films on advertising and marketing, and many other consumer-education materials.

As a political cause, the consumer and environmental movement emerged with advocates such as Ralph Nader, a lawyer who became widely known for his book *Unsafe At Any Speed*, which described safety defects in General Motors' Corvair. Nader investigated and attacked the entire automobile industry for its failure to build safe cars. His work helped bring about the National Traffic and Motor Vehicle Safety Act of 1966.

A few years later, Nader formed a group called the Center for the Study of Responsive Law that included young lawyers and graduate students in law, who were often referred to as "Nader's Raiders." The center investigated industries, government organizations, and labor unions and called attention to illegal or negligent practices that could harm consumers and workers.

The Nader group paid particular attention to government agencies that were set up to protect consumers. Investigators found that little had been done to guard the public from marketplace fraud, environmental pollution, and health hazards. Nader claimed the agencies were influenced by and catered to the very industries they were supposed to govern and regulate.

Some of the lawsuits brought by the Nader group forced government agencies to take action on consumer complaints and encouraged many other consumer groups to organize. These volunteer groups also pressured for new legislation, particularly laws that would prevent hazards to public health and the environment and laws that would prevent discrimination against members of minority groups.

CONSUMER GROUPS

Hundreds of consumer action groups have been established at the national level and in every state since the 1960s. Some deal with general consumer education and protection, while others are organized to address specific consumer problems such as those that may occur because of misleading or false advertising.

Many newspapers and local radio and TV stations sponsor "Action Lines"—columns or programs that address consumer complaints. Adverse publicity about a business can be effective in resolving problems, because businesses do not want a reputation for dishonesty or for selling poor quality merchandise or performing shoddy service.

Still other organizations that can be of help to consumers are trade groups or organizations that are part of a particular industry. Many of these organizations deal with advertising abuses. For example, the Council of Better Business Bureaus, a national organization, includes an advertising division that monitors advertising for abuses and investigates complaints about misleading and deceptive advertising. The council is one of the sponsors of the National Advertising Review Board (NARB), an advertising industry group that was set up in 1971 to establish guidelines for the self-regulation of ads. The NARB also encourages complaints from consumers about deceptive or misleading advertising.

Ads that come to the attention of the NARB are reviewed to determine whether they contain false or highly exaggerated statements, misleading price claims, unfair comparisons with competing products or services, claims that are not supported by sufficient facts, or statements or photos that are considered offensive to the general public.

Broadcasters, too, have regulations about the kind of advertising they will accept. Major TV networks preview thousands of product commercials each year. CBS, for example, reviewed about 50,000 product commercials in

1989. Networks check for fraudulent claims for products and unfair comparisons with competing products. Most commercials are accepted, but about 2 or 3 percent are rejected outright and others have to be revised, usually with evidence or statistics to substantiate claims.[4]

GOVERNMENT REGULATORS

Because of efforts by volunteers as well as legislators concerned about protecting consumers, hundreds of federal, state, and local laws and regulations now guard against corrupt dealings in the marketplace. In addition, the Civil Rights Act of 1968 includes protective measures for consumers who may be discriminated against because of color, national origin, religious affiliation, or gender. For example, the Fair Housing section of the law prohibits advertisers from limiting real estate buyers or renters to certain groups or indicating discriminatory practices. Ads in classified sections of newspapers usually carry a notice such as the following:

Rentals 500	APA/ UNF
ALL REAL ESTATE advertised herein is subject to the Federal Fair Housing Act which makes it illegal to advertise "any preference, limitation, or discrimination based on race, color, religion, sex, handicap, familial status, or national origin, or intention to make any such preference, limitation, or discrimination. We will not knowingly accept any advertising for real estate which is in violation of the law. All persons are hereby informed that all dwellings advertised are available on an equal opportunity basis. Persons having reason to believe they have been discriminated against on the basis of race, religion, color, sex, familial status, national origin or ancestry, or handicap may contact the South Bend Human Rights Commission at 284-9355.	A 2 be area, mo., lec posit, n BLA(1-2 bed E. Jeff ceptin cants. BOTT 4 room bookc(utilitie CHAR/ down/ no sr CHA apr uti pe

The Federal Trade Commission (FTC) is responsible for regulating most of the marketing practices in the United States, and many people in the advertising industry believe the agency's power and the widespread publicity surrounding cases it investigates effectively prevent frauds in the marketplace. Founded in 1914, the FTC is composed of five commissioners, appointed by the president of the United States, who oversee a number of divisions. The agency's Consumer Protection Division, for example, is responsible for enforcing laws and regulations designed to prevent price-fixing, dishonest packaging and selling, and deceptive advertising. The FTC also enforces laws dealing with health and safety issues in advertising. One example described for *Money* magazine is "the heavy telemarketing of home water purifiers" under FTC investigation. As FTC head Janet Steiger explained in an interview for the magazine:

> For $400 or $500, folks buy filters for their kitchen faucets that are virtually worthless. Some may even be harmful because they add dangerous chemicals to the water you drink. The marketers frequently like to use scare tactics. They'll say, for instance, that the U.S. Government just passed a law saying that every home must have a water purifier by 1992. There is no such law.[5]

The FTC also enforces the 1970 law that bans cigarette advertising on TV and requires that cigarette ads in newspapers and magazines and on billboards, as well as on cigarette packages, carry warnings like these about the health hazards of smoking.

SURGEON GENERAL'S WARNING: Smoking
By Pregnant Women May Result in Fetal
Injury, Premature Birth, And Low Birth Weight.

SURGEON GENERAL'S WARNING: Cigarette
Smoke Contains Carbon Monoxide.

SURGEON GENERAL'S WARNING: Quitting Smoking
Now Greatly Reduces Serious Risks to Your Health.

SURGEON GENERAL'S WARNING: Smoking
Causes Lung Cancer, Heart Disease,
Emphysema, And May Complicate Pregnancy.

Other consumer-protection laws that come under the jurisdiction of the FTC include those requiring honest labeling of fabrics, furs, and furniture materials. Clothing labels, for example, must tell exactly what fabrics garments are made of, such as 100 percent wool, or 60 percent cotton and 40 percent polyester. Labels on natural and artificial leather and fur goods must indicate their sources. Furniture must also carry tags that describe the materials used in their construction. A desk could be made of oak wood, for example, or made of a manufactured material finished to look like oak. Such regulations are designed to protect consumers from manufacturers who might falsely label synthetic goods—fake furs for instance—and then advertise their products as the real thing.

The Food and Drug Administration (FDA) is the federal agency "whose scientists approve the safety and effectiveness of drugs and medical devices, safeguard the wholesomeness of the nation's food supply, and ensure the safety of cosmetics." As the agency explained, it regulates goods produced and distributed by 89,400 companies and during an average year inspects about 20,000 of the firms, about 400 of which are in other nations. FDA investigators also annually "review about 1.5 million imported goods, and conduct 100,000 examinations at the wharves. In addition, agency scientists each year analyze 75,000 product samples."[6]

The FDA makes certain that cosmetics are produced under sanitary conditions and are safe for consumers. It also regulates food labels, except for meat and poultry, which are under the jurisdiction of the U.S. Department of Agriculture. In addition, the FDA makes sure that warnings against possible hazards to health and safety appear on drugs and other products.

The Consumer Product Safety Commission (CPSC) is another important protection agency. It operates a product safety hot line (800-638-2772), which consumers can call toll free with complaints about household products that can or do cause injuries or to report product-related injuries. CPSC frequently receives calls that must be referred to other agencies—for example, a food or cosmetic problem would be referred to the FDA. Problems with auto safety would be handled by the National Highway Traffic Safety Administration whose toll-free hot line is 800-424-9393. CPSC has jurisdiction over such products as household appliances, bicycles, toys, and child-resistant packaging— packages designed so that young children cannot open them easily.

How are consumer complaints handled? "We take complaints and turn these over to our technical staff," a representative at CPSC explained. "The technicians determine whether or not further investigation is warranted. Even if action is not taken immediately, it is important that consumers register complaints," the CPSC representative stressed. "Frequently we are criticized for not acting fast enough, but we may have only a few isolated complaints about a product and they may not indicate that further investigation is necessary. But when complaints show a pattern of problems or that people nationwide are reporting on hazardous conditions related to a specific product, then the agency is more likely to begin investigations."[7]

If you have a complaint about fraudulent materials sent through the mail, the U.S. Postal Service can help with the problem. The Postal Service also handles complaints about contests and prizes that are part of sales campaigns conducted by mail and problems with unsolicited mail, pornography, and hazardous materials sent through the mail.

The U.S. Office of Consumer Affairs publishes a *Consumer's Resource Handbook* that provides guidance and resources for many consumer problems. It also lists federal, state, and local government agencies for consumer affairs, which can provide some protection for consumers, too. The handbook is available free from the Consumer Information Center, Pueblo, Colorado 81009. The center operates offices in twenty-one cities and responds to inquiries about services provided by federal agencies and departments. In addition, the center publishes a free *Consumer Information Catalog* that lists free and low-cost booklets and pamphlets of consumer interest published by the federal government.

Other federal agencies that offer consumer-protection services include the U.S. Department of Agriculture, which has over 3,000 offices nationwide and deals with problems related to a vast array of consumer issues, from food production and assistance to pesticide use to agricultural marketing research. The Environmental Protection Agency, as its name implies, was set up to protect consumers from environmental hazards such as air and water pollution and hazardous waste.

States also have set up their own consumer agencies, known by such titles as the Department of Consumer Affairs, Department of Consumer Protection, Governor's Council for Consumer Affairs, or Governor's Office of Consumer Affairs. Consumer complaints, particularly in regard to fraud, also may be handled by a state office of the attorney general, which has the legal power to take cases to court to try to correct consumer problems. So does a county district attorney's office or a city attorney's office. Addresses for local and state consumer agencies are listed in telephone directories and also in consumer directories in public libraries. City and state government officials also are able to direct people to agencies that will help with consumer problems.

CHAPTER TEN

SMART SHOPPING

In spite of the laws, regulators, and citizen watchdog groups, it is unrealistic to expect that all marketers, advertisers, or advertising professionals will be absolutely honest. A society can never be protected from every crook and con artist, as there are always dishonest people around who will risk fines and jail sentences to beguile, hustle, or cheat others.

Yet it is important to remember that the vast majority of businesses that advertise their goods and services are not trying to cheat you. Business owners just want you to buy from them rather than from their competitors, and their advertising is designed with that aim in mind. Since there are many choices in U.S. marketplaces, and many advertisers who would like you to buy, you may want to sharpen your buying skills so that you buy only what you need or want and can afford.

BUYING BARGAINS

Glance through a newspaper, walk through a mall, push a cart through a supermarket and you are likely to see advertising for special items on sale. "Buy one, get one free," is a common marketing technique in some supermarkets, and there is little doubt that you can save money by buying two for the price of one. Using cents-off coupons from direct-mail advertisers or from newspapers and magazines can help cut costs, too. So can buying generic brands— items packaged in containers with plain labels that only describe the contents.

Store brands, or products packaged specifically for supermarkets, are usually identical or almost the same as name brands but cost much less because name-brand products are supported by national advertising, which is expensive and adds to the cost of goods.

Yet no matter what the bargain price, you do not save money if you buy products only because they are "good buys." Beware of buying items that you do not need or do not really want. Suppose you intend to buy a package of envelopes and they are advertised "2 for $1.00." Do you really save money if you buy two when you only need one package?

Also guard against buying on impulse. Merchants frequently place bargain items in strategic places, usually near the main entrance in a department store, or at the checkout counter in a supermarket. Or there may be displays of goods in the aisles, forcing you to stop to look and perhaps buy impulsively. You might also be tempted to buy items displayed along with products you intended to purchase. Perhaps you would buy snacks, for example, if they were displayed beside soft drinks, or a vegetable dip that might be sitting conveniently in a bin beside the carrots, celery, and broccoli. Resisting such selling techniques (unless you truly want the product) is one of the ways you can be a smart shopper.

In a supermarket, another safeguard against buying more than you need or more than you can afford is to make a list before you go shopping and get only the listed items. Eat before you shop so you will not buy more food than you need simply because you are hungry. Also carry a small calculator. By adding up items as you select them you will be forewarned if your total bill is going to exceed what you plan to spend.

Another precaution: Do not stay in a supermarket too long. Market researchers have found that consumers who linger beyond the time it takes to select weekly groceries are likely to buy more than they had planned. Experts also say that consumers spend more money in a store that is pleasant and fun to be in.

COMPARISON SHOPPING

Many experienced and prudent shoppers spend time comparing goods and services to get the "best buy." Sometimes you can compare by checking out newspaper ads for similar products or services. Perhaps, for example, you can buy a jacket you want from a store that is selling it for several dollars less than the place where you regularly shop. But you might also have to consider where the store is. If you have to travel miles to get a bargain, you might spend whatever you save on the jacket for transportation.

You also should check quality and durability when you are buying such products as clothing, furniture, sports equipment, and other goods that you expect to last for more than a few months. Maintenance is also a factor. Consider that jacket you want. Perhaps there are many of a similar type to choose from, but each might be made from different materials. If you narrow your choice between two jackets that are the same price but one can be washed and the other must be dry-cleaned, which is the best buy? Dry-cleaning a jacket usually costs more than washing it, so you might opt for the washable jacket to save on maintenance costs.

To compare packaged foods, you should check the unit price rather than simply the size of packages. For example, you might choose between two different-sized packages of candy bars—one with five bars, the other with ten. The smaller package costs $1.98 while the larger is $2.98. If you want to know which is the best buy, divide the price of a pack by the number of candy bars in it. The bars in the smaller pack cost almost forty cents apiece and those in the larger one are about thirty cents apiece, so the larger pack is the better buy.

Many times unit prices for packaged foods are shown on store shelves, so you do not have to make the calculations yourself. You can quickly see which size of the same product is the best buy. One seventeen-year-old shopper in Indianapolis who, like a large number of other teenagers, buys the family groceries each week, said that she always reads labels carefully to see which package is the best buy. "Sometimes the large can is 20 cents less," she noted.[1]

In some instances, though, the largest package may not be the least expensive, even though such terms as "Economy Size," "Family Size," or "Giant Size" are on the container. These terms frequently are used to attract buyers who hope to save money. But it might be less costly to buy two small containers than one large one.

In a recent development, some food processors have been putting less of their products in new packages, but are not reducing the prices, or they are increasing the amount slightly and creating much larger packages. A large new package tends to give the impression that there is more product inside than was inside the older package. Kellogg, for one, created a "New Larger Size" NutriGrain Wheat Cereal. The new box is 15 percent larger than the old one, but the weight of the product itself was increased by less than 2 percent. New York's commissioner of Consumer Affairs says that such practices are "sneaky and misleading" ways to raise prices without actually changing the price tag.[2]

Even packages that appear to be the same in size may have less product. Star-Kist tuna, for example, reduced the size of its 6½-ounce can of tuna fish to 6⅛ ounce, reducing the can itself by a barely noticeable $\frac{1}{16}$ inch. The price did not drop accordingly, however.

Consumer Reports has published information from readers on similar practices. One reader reported that the Near East company reduced its Rice Pilaf Mix by one ounce but did not change its package or price. Another said that she bought calcium tablets from a drugstore chain and paid $1.09 for sixty tablets; then a few weeks later she bought the same number of tablets packaged in a larger bottle for $1.99. To repeat, then, it is the unit price rather than package size that consumers should check to determine the best buy.[3]

You should also compare ingredients on food labels. Federal law requires that the contents of food products be listed according to the amount of each ingredient, the largest quantity first. In other words, a label on a can of one brand of chicken noodle soup might list the broth first, because it is the major ingredient. Noodles might be listed next, then chicken, then spices, and so on. Compare this list with one from another brand of the same kind of soup. Are the ingredients equal? What about the individual prices?

CHECKING OUT ADVERTISING CLAIMS

So you have read the ads or have seen the commercials that all but promise you the world. To find out whether the claims are valid, you can read what independent researchers learn about goods and services. Reports of studies (many conducted by Consumers Union and others by university researchers or consumer action groups) frequently are published in magazines and newspapers. The Consumers Union publication *Zillions* also reports on tests of advertising claims for such products as athletic shoes and video games.

You can also do some testing on your own. Suppose you want to find out whether a particular soap leaves the tub or sink film-free or whether one cleansing powder cleans better than another. You simply do what some ads advise: try the products and see for yourself.

There are many inexpensive experiments that can help you determine the qualities of products. Perhaps you want to compare brands of paper towels. Which one "absorbs better" or is "softer" or "stronger"? You might want to test whether softness has anything to do with the way a towel absorbs. Is strength an important factor in regard to paper towels? You might even ask yourself whether you really need paper towels, especially if these products are not made from recycled materials and use up valuable resources. Would it be wiser to buy reusable cloth towels or sponges?

You can check out some product claims with simple surveys of friends and relatives. Ask them to rate products they have used. They may also rate services they have received. If someone you know well recommends a new restaurant, a garage with a "good mechanic," or a shop where hair stylists know the latest fashions, you are likely to try these places. After trying recommended products or services, you can decide for yourself which are satisfactory and worth paying for in the future.

CAUTION, YOU MAY BE AN ADVERTISEMENT

Are you wearing a T-shirt or sweatshirt that advertises a product like Coke or a TV show like "The Simpsons?" Do you always buy brand name clothing? Is it important that you look and act like the actors and actresses you see on TV commercials? Would you buy a product just because a celebrity endorsed it?

Many consumers are walking advertisements for some products because they like to display name-brand goods that are linked with the famous or with those who have "made it" economically and socially. So one of the basic questions you might ask yourself as a smart shopper is the question posed in chapter 5: "Why buy?" Is it to satisfy your needs or desires or to conform to advertising images?

In the years ahead, you can be certain that hundreds of thousands of messages will be coming your way urging you to buy. But what, when, where, and how you spend your money are choices you should be free to make. It is up to you to use that freedom to develop shopping skills and to be a wise consumer.

SOURCE NOTES

CHAPTER ONE

1. Eric Clark, *The Want Makers* (New York: Penguin Books, 1988), 14.
2. Stan Rapp and Tom Collins, *The Great Marketing Turnaround* (Englewood Cliffs, N.J.: Prentice-Hall, 1990), 27.   3. Personal Interview.
4. As quoted by Eric Clark, *The Want Makers* (New York: Penguin Books, 1988), 15.   5. Stephen Garey, "How Ads Reflect Our Consumer Society," *Media&Values* (Summer 1990), 21.

CHAPTER TWO

1. Henry Sampson, *History of Advertising* (London: Chatto & Windus, 1933), 19.   2. James Playsted Wood, *The Story of Advertising* (New York: The Ronald Press, 1958), Chapter 2.   3. Harry Golden, *The Forgotten Pioneer* (New York: The World Publishing Company, 1963). Also see: Penrose Scull, *From Peddlers to Merchant Princes* (Chicago and New York: Follett Publishing Company, 1967).   4. Jerrold K. Footlick, "What Happened to the Family?" *Newsweek* Special Edition (Winter-Spring 1990), 16–17.   5. Stan Rapp and Tom Collins, *The Great Marketing Turnaround* (Englewood Cliffs, N.J.: Prentice-Hall, 1990), 17.

CHAPTER THREE

1. Peter F. Eder, "Advertising and Mass Marketing," *The Futurist* (May-June 1990), 39. Also see: Christopher Warden, "Power to the

Consumer," *Consumers' Research* (June 1989), 19.   **2.** Personal interview.   **3.** Personal interview.   **4.** Bruce Horovitz, "Trying to Get a Better Picture of How People Feel About an Ad," *Los Angeles Times* (February 6, 1990), D6.   **5.** Eric Clark, *The Want Makers: Inside the World of Advertising* (New York and London: Penguin Books, 1988), 63.   **6.** Stan Rapp and Tom Collins, *The Great Marketing Turnaround* (Englewood Cliffs, N.J.: Prentice-Hall, 1990), Chapter 4.   **7.** "Total National Ad Spending by Category and Media," *Advertising Age* (September 25, 1991), 8.   **8.** Personal Interview.   **9.** Rapp and Collins, 126.   **10.** James U. McNeal, *Children as Consumers* (Lexington, Mass.: D.C. Heath and Company, 1987), 110.   **11.** Jill Smolowe, "Read This!!!!!!!!" *Time* (November 26, 1990), 63.   **12.** Amy Bernstein, "Wish Book," *U.S. News & World Report* (February 25, 1991), 14.   **13.** Leonard Sloane, "Despite Complaints, Solicitation by Phone or Mail is Growing," *The New York Times* (September 1, 1990), 16.   **14.** Christopher Warden, "Power to the Consumer," *Consumers' Research* (June 1990), 19.   **15.** David Schreiber, "Advertising Wars. Is It What You Say or How You Say It?" *The Elkhart Truth Business Report* (January 15, 1991), 3.   **16.** Hunter Hastings, "Mixing Markets," *Vital Speeches of the Day* (August 1, 1990), 615–617.

CHAPTER FOUR

1. Robert B. Settle and Pamela L. Alreck, *Why They Buy* (New York: John Wiley & Sons, 1989), 7.   **2.** Karen Springen and Annetta Miller, "Sequels for the Shelf," *Newsweek* (July 9, 1990), 42.   **3.** Bernice Kanner, "From the Subliminal to the Ridiculous," *New York* (December 4, 1989), 18–22. Also see: Jo Anna Natale, "Are You Open to Suggestion?" *Psychology Today* (September 1988), 28–30. Also see: Herbert Rotfeld, "Subliminal Foolishness," *Los Angeles Times* (April 1, 1986), Metro Section, 5.   **4.** Carol Moog *"Are They Selling Her Lips?"* (New York: William Morrow and Company, 1990), 142–143.   **5.** Robert D. Ekelund, Jr. and David S. Saurman, *Advertising and the Market Process* (San Francisco: Pacific Research Institute for Public Policy, 1988), 112

CHAPTER FIVE

1. Peter Newcomb, "Hey, Dude, Let's Consume," *Forbes* (June 11, 1990), 126.   **2.** As reported by Associated Press in June 1990.   **3.** Doris Walsh, "The Big Giveaway," *American Demographics* (June 1988), 60.   **4.** Annetta Miller and Dody Tsiantar, "The Kids Play—And You Pay," *Newsweek* (November 12, 1990), 52.   **5.** As quoted by

Katherine and Richard Greene, "Special Redbook Report: The Shocking Statistics, *Redbook* (March 1990), 93.   **6.** Walter Goodman, "Cautionary Guide for Little Customers," *The New York Times* (December 3, 1989), H33.   **7.** "Welcome to the Clubs," *Zillions* (December 1990–January 1991), 22–24.   **8.** Bernice Kanner, "Courting the Tweens," *New York* (March 26, 1990), 19.   **9.** CU news release, July 17, 1990 and phone interview March 1991. Also see: "Selling to Children," *Consumer Reports* (August 1990), 518–521.   **10.** Iris Cohen Selinger, "Advertisers Go to School on Scholastic," *AdWeek* (June 25, 1990), 17. **11.** Joshua Hammer, "A Golden Boy's Toughest Sell," *Newsweek* (February 19, 1990), 52–53. Also see: Walter Goodman, "TV News in Schools: Which Channel, if Any?" *The New York Times* (March 14, 1990).   **12.** Patricia Sellers, "The ABC'S of Marketing to Kids," *Fortune* (May 8, 1989), 118–120.   **13.** Paul Farhi, "Spring-Break Beer Messages Draw Fire," *Washington Post* (March 28, 1990).   **14.** Evelyn C. White, "Study Rips Ties of Beer Makers to Auto Racing," *San Francisco Chronicle* (May 15, 1990).   **15.** As quoted by Tom Morganthau, "Sullivan: Bush's Aide Makes Waves," *Newsweek* (March 5, 1990), 19. **16.** As quoted by Kim Foltz, "Old Joe Is Paying Off for Camel," *The New York Times* (August 7, 1990).   **17.** Mark Green, "Let's Stop Selling Cancer to Children," *The New York Times* (July 1, 1990). **18.** George F. Will, "Tobacco's Targets," *Washington Post* (February 25, 1990).   **19.** As quoted in AP wire story, January 25, 1990. **20.** Mireya Navarro, "Tobacco and Alcohol Manufacturers Find Minorities Are Growing Wary," *The New York Times* (August 8, 1990). **21.** Bruce Maxwell and Michael Jacobson, *Marketing Disease to Hispanics* (Washington, D.C.: Center for Science in the Public Interest, September 1989), ix.   **22.** Annetta Miller with Dody Tsiantar, Karen Springen, Mary Hager, and Kate Robins, "Oat-Bran Heartburn," *Newsweek* (January 29, 1990), 50–52.   **23.** "Food Labeling," *Facts on File* (November 2, 1990), 816.   **24.** Ronald D. Knutson with C. Robert Taylor, John B. Penson, and Edward G. Smith. "Pesticide-Free Equals Higher Food Prices." *Consumer Research* (November 1990), 33–35. **25.** Board on Agriculture of the National Research Council. *Alternative Agriculture* (Washington, DC: National Academy Press, 1989), 3–23. Also see: Kathlyn Gay, *Cleaning Nature Naturally* (New York: Walker and Company, 1991), Chapter 4.

CHAPTER SIX

1. Gordon W. Allport, *The Nature of Prejudice*, Tenth Edition (Reading, Mass.: Addison-Wesley, 1987), pp. 29–40.   **2.** Ibid. Also see: John Appel and Selma Appel, "Anti-Semitism in American Caricature" *Society*

(November-December 1986), 78-83. Also see: Joseph Boskin, *Sambo: The Rise and Demise of an American Jester* (New York and Oxford: Oxford University Press, 1986). Also see: Kathlyn Gay, *Bigotry* (Hillside, N.J.: Enslow Publishers, 1989), Chapter 3. Also see: Carol Moog, *"Are They Selling Her Lips?" Advertising and Identity* (New York: William Morrow and Company, 1990, Chapter 9. **3.** Personal interview. **4.** As quoted by John Schrag, "Lily-White Christmas," *Williamette Week* (December 13-19, 1990, 1, 11–12. **5.** Ellen Goodman, "It's Equal Rites Awards Time Again," *Boston Globe* (August 26, 1990). **6.** David B. Wolfe, *Serving the Ageless Market* (New York: McGraw-Hill, 1990), 12, 37. **7.** Melinda Beck, "Going for the Gold," *Newsweek* (April 23, 1990), 74. **8.** As quoted by M.W. Newman, "Sign City," Chicago *Sunday Sun-Times* (March 22, 1981). **9.** Ed McMahon, "Tress Vs. Billboards," *American Forests* (September-October 1990), 49. Also see: Douglas Fulmer, "Sweeping Billboard Reforms Proposed," *E Magazine* (November-December 1990), 9–10. **10.** Eleanor Randolph, "Extra! Extra! Who Cares? Newspapers Face the Incredible Shrinking Reader," *Washington Post* (April 1, 1990). **11.** Mortimer B. Zuckerman, "The Illiteracy Epidemic," *U.S. News & World Report* (June 12, 1989), 72. **12.** Eric Clark, *The Want Makers* (New York: Penguin Books, 1988), 341. **13.** Kim Foltz, "Magazine Industry Bracing for Shakeout as Ads Drop," *The New York Times* (April 30, 1990). **14.** Bob Schulberg, *Radio Advertising* (Lincolnwood, Ill.: NTC Publishing Group, 1989), Chapter 1. **15.** John Sims, "What's With Those 'Amazing' TV Ads?" *Money* (August 1990), 30. Also see: Sherri Vazzano, "TV Ads Policing Own Act," *Chicago Tribune* (November 23, 1990). Also see: Laurel Pallock, "Beware of the 'Infomercial,' " *San Francisco Chronicle* (November 28, 1990). **16.** Consumers Union: *Selling America's Kids* (Mount Vernon, New York: Consumers Union Education Services, 1990), 14. **17.** Harold A. Shoup, "Letters" (regular column). *Newsweek* (February 19, 1990), 14. **18.** O. Lee Reed, "Reading the Tea Leaves: Future Regulation of Product-Extrinsic Advertising," *Business Horizons* (September-October 1990), 88–92. **19.** "Smoking 'Em Out," *The Economist* (September 15, 1990), 83. **20.** Gallup Organization poll July 6 through July 8, 1990, released July 18, 1990.

CHAPTER SEVEN

1. James E. Burke, "Breaking a Habit of Mind; The Right Messages Can Change Attitudes Toward Drug Use," *Washington Post* (November 11, 1990). **2.** Personal interview. **3.** Herb Chao Gunther, "The Difference Between Commercial Mail and Non-Profit Mail," *Utne Reader*

(November-December 1990), 56. **4.** Michael Weisskopf, "From Fringe to Political Mainstream; Environmentalists Set Policy Agenda," *Washington Post* (April 19, 1990). Also see: Joan Goldstein, *Demanding Clean Food and Water* (New York: Plenum Publishing Corporation, 1990), 68–71. Also see: "Too Much Fuss About Pesticides? *Consumer Reports* (October 1989), 655–658. **5.** Joseph D. Rosen, "Much Ado About Alar," *Issues in Science and Technology* (Fall 1990) 85–90. Also see: "Does Everything Cause Cancer?" *Consumers' Research* (May 1989), 11–13. Also see: Bruce Ames, "Be Most Wary of Nature's Own Pesticides," *Consumers' Research* (May 1989), 13–14. **6.** Joan Goldstein, *Demanding Clean Food and Water* (New York: Plenum Publishing Corporation, 1990), 68–71. **7.** Julie Liesse, "Line Between Public Service, Paid Ads Blurs," *Advertising Age* (October 8, 1990), 28. **8.** "Directory of Who's Who in Environmental Marketing," *Advertising Age* (January 29, 1991), 38–45. **9.** Judann Dagnoli, "Green Buys Taking Root," *Advertising Age* (September 3, 1990), 27. **10.** Patricia W. Hamilton, "Green, Gray and Tired of Glitz," *D&B Reports* (July-August 1990), 27. **11.** Laurie Freeman, "Procter & Gamble," *Advertising Age* (January 29, 1991), 16, 34. **12.** As quoted by Easy Klein, "The Selling of the Green," *D&B Reports* (September-October 1990), 35. **13.** Jennifer Lawrence and Steven W. Colford, "Green Guidelines Are the Next Step," *Advertising Age* (January 29, 1991), 28. **14.** David S. Broder, "Mudball Politics," *Washington Post* (November 4, 1990). **15.** Survey conducted by Yankelovich Clancy Shulman, October 15 through October 17, 1990, released October 22, 1990. **16.** Bob Garfield, "Let Voters Take Warning: Political Advertising In This Country is a Travesty," *Advertising Age* (November 6, 1990), 29.

CHAPTER EIGHT

1. William Lutz, *Doublespeak* (New York: HarperCollins Publishers, 1990), 86–87. **2.** Ibid, 102. **3.** Stuart Silverstein, "Big Discounts May Put Some Stores in Red," *Los Angeles Times* (December 5, 1990). **4.** Don McLeod, "Fund-Raisers' Ploy Taps Credit Cards," *AARP Bulletin* (December 1990), 5. Also see "Selling It," *Consumer Reports* (November 1990), 771. **5.** "Bad Apples: In the Executive Suite," *Consumer Reports* (May 1989), 294–296. **6.** Ibid. **7.** James S. Benson. "FDA Enforcement Activities Protect Public," *FDA Consumer* (January-February 1991), 7–8. **8.** Victor Galvin, UPI General News Story, July 6, 1990. **9.** Raymond Serafin and Jennifer Lawrence, "Volvo Parent Seizes Control of Inquiry," *Advertising Age* (November 19, 1990), 1, 54. Also see: Paul Farhi, "Ad Makers Enter 'Hall of Shame,' " *Washington Post* (December 11, 1990).

CHAPTER NINE

1. Andrew Eiler, *The Consumer Protection Manual* (New York: Facts on File Publications, 1934), 36. Also see: *Reader's Digest Consumer Adviser* (Pleasantville, N.Y.: The Reader's Digest Association, 1989), 9. **2.** Consumers Union editors, *Testing: Behind the Scenes at Consumer Reports 1936–1986*, Introduction by Walter Kronkite (Mount Vernon, N.Y: Consumers Union, 1986), xi–xii. **3.** Correspondence from Peter Spencer, Executive Editor, *Consumers' Research*, February 1991. **4.** Bernice Kanner, "To Tell the Truth," *New York* (October 15, 1990), 22–24. Also see: Paul Taylor, "Political Pitches Called Insult to Advertising," *Washington Post* (March 25, 1990). **5.** Miriam Leuchter, "A Scam Alert from the Top Shopping Cop," *Money* (November 1990), 28–29. **6.** James S. Benson, "FDA Enforcement Activities Protect Public," *FDA Consumer* (January-February 1991), 7. **7.** Phone interview.

CHAPTER TEN

1. As quoted by Donna Segal, "Teens In Grocery Land," *The Indianapolis Star* (January 10, 1990). **2.** As quoted by David E. Kalish in an Associated Press news story, January 6, 1991. **3.** "Selling It" column, *Consumer Reports* (January, April, June, August, September, and November 1990 issues).

FOR FURTHER READING

BOOKS

American Bar Association. *Your Legal Guide to Consumer Credit*. Chicago, Ill.: American Bar Association Public Education Division, 1988.

Council on Economic Priorities. *Shopping for a Better World*. New York: Ballantine Books, 1990.

Editors of Consumer Reports Books with Monte Florman. *1,001 Helpful Tips, Facts & Hints from Consumer Reports*. Mount Vernon, NY: Consumers Union, 1989.

Gill, Kay, and Robert Wilson, eds. *Consumer Sourcebook*. Fifth Edition. Detroit: Gale Research Company, 1988.

Gold, Phillip. *Advertising, Politics, and American Culture*. New York: Paragon House Publishers, 1987.

Goldstein, Sue. *Secrets From the Underground Shopper*. Dallas: Taylor Publishing Company, 1986.

Kozol, Jonathan. *Illiterate America*. New York: Anchor/Doubleday, 1985.

Makower, Joel, John Elkington, and Julia Hailes. *The Green Consumer*. New York: Penguin Books, 1990.

Maxwell Associates and Editors of the Reader's Digest Association. *Reader's Digest Consumer Adviser: An Action Guide to Your Rights*. Pleasantville, N.Y.: The Reader's Digest Association, 1989.

Ogilvy, David. *Confessions of an Advertising Man*. New York: Atheneum, 1988.

O'Toole, John. *The Trouble With Advertising: A View From the Inside*. New York: Times Books/Random House, 1985.

Perlongo, Bob, comp. *Early American Advertising*. New York: Art Direction Book Company, 1985.

Presby, Frank. *The History and Development of Advertising*. New York: Doubleday, Doran & Company, 1929.

Strasser, Susan, *Satisfaction Guaranteed: The Making of the American Mass Market*: New York: Pantheon Books, 1989.

U.S. Office of Consumer Affairs. *Consumer's Resource Handbook*. Pueblo, Colo.: Consumer Information Center, 1990.

Weiss, Ann. *The School on Madison Avenue: Advertising and What It Teaches*. New York: Dutton, 1980.

PERIODICALS

"A 'Black' Cigarette Goes Up in Smoke." *Newsweek*, January 29, 1990, 54.

Alter, Johnathan. "The Media Mud Squad." *Newsweek*, October 29, 1990, 37.

Appel, John, and Selma Appel. "Anti-Semitism in American Caricature." *Society*, November-December 1986, 78–83.

Asimov, Nanette. "Consumer Politics; There's Big Power in the Boycott." *San Francisco Chronicle*, October 2, 1990, A1.

Associated Press. "Anti-Drug Ads Help Curb Abuse, Survey Finds." *San Francisco Chronicle*, January 30, 1990.

Bahouth, Peter, and Andre Carothers. "In Defense of Junk Mail: Mailbox As Public Square." *Utne Reader*, November-December 1990, 55–58.

Beckett, Jamie. "New Marketing Study Targets Teenagers." *San Francisco Chronicle*, April 17, 1989.

Begley, Sharon, with Mary Hager and Lynda Wright. "The Selling of Earth Day." *Newsweek*, March 26, 1990, 60–61.

Bellafante, Ginia. "Organic Foods: Are You Getting What You Pay For?" *Garbage*, November-December 1989, 38–42.

Berry, Kathleen M. "The Snap Has Turned to Slog." *The New York Times*, November 18, 1990.

Brown, Donna. "Let the Buyer Beware." *Management Review*, June 1990, 18–21.

Chase, Dennis. "P&G Gets Top Marks in AA Survey." *Advertising Age*, January 29, 1991, 8–10.

Christian, Sue Ellen. "Organic Food-Labeling Rules Given Teeth by New U.S. Law." *Los Angeles Times*, November 15, 1990.

Cowan, Andy. "A White Christmas, Fine; White Catalogues, No." *Los Angeles Times*, December 9, 1990.

Cronin, Mary and William McWhirter. "Volunteer Vice Squad." *Time*, April 23, 1990, 60–61.

Dagnoli, Judann. "Consumers Union Hits Kids' Advertising." *Advertising Age*, July 23, 1990, 4.

Davis, Susan E. "Prefab News." *Technology Review*, October 6, 1989, 6–7.

"Do Good Things Come in Green Packages? *Garbage*, July-August 1990, 80.

"Does the Government Have a Role in Product Safety?" *Consumers' Research*. February 1990, 10–13, 29.

Dold, Catherine A. "Green to Go." *American Health*, April 1990, 47–54.

Endicott, R. Craig, and Keven Brown. "Top 100 Boosts and Ad Spending 6.4% to Almost $34 Billion." *Advertising Age*, September 26, 1990, 1.

Engelhardt, Tom. "Saturday Morning Fever." *Mother Jones*, September 1986, 39–48.

Fisher, Christy. "Marketing to Hispanics." *Advertising Age*, October 15, 1990, 42.

Gallagher, John E., with John F. McDonald and Don Winbush. "Under Fire from All Sides." *Time*, March 5, 1990, 41.

Gamarekian, Barbara. "Ads Aimed at Children Restricted." *The New York Times*, October 18, 1990.

Garfield, Bob. "Beware: Green Overkill." *Advertising Age*, January 29, 1991.

Graves, Bill. "Students Tune in to TV Program." *The Oregonian*, September 18, 1990.

Hall, Trish. "The Young Are Getting and Spending, Too." *The New York Times*, August 23, 1990.

Hawken, Paul. "The Junk (Mail) Stops Here." *Utne Reader*, November-December 1990, 51–54.

Jay, Leslie. "Green About the Tills: Markets Discover the Eco-Consumer." *Management Review*, June 1990, 24–28.

Kanner Bernice. "The Secret Life of the Female Consumer." *Working Woman*, December 1990, 69–71.

———. "To Tell the Truth." *New York*, October 15, 1990, 22–24.

"L.A. Gear The Inside Story." *Zillions Consumer Reports for Kids*, October-November 1990, 16–18.

Latimer, Leah Y. "Effort Aims to Shock Youngsters Into Abstinence." *Washington Post*, August 7, 1989.

Lazarus, George. "On Marketing—Arm & Hammer Shows Some Teeth." *Chicago Tribune*, September 6, 1990.

"Let the Supermarket-Shopper Beware." *Modern Maturity*, April-May 1990, 9.

Levin, Gary. "Negative Ads Win on Election Day '90." *Advertising Age*, November 12, 1990, 3.

Liesse, Julie. "KGF Taps Data Base to Target Consumers." *Advertising Age*, October 8, 1990, 3.

Liesse, Julie, and Steven W. Colford. "Marketers Like New Label Law." *Advertising Age*, October 29, 1990, 67.

Mabry, Marcus, with Daniel Glick and Shawn D. Lewis. "Fighting Ads in the Inner City." *Newsweek*, February 5, 1990, 46.

Maclean, John N. "Oil Industry Fights Image, Supply Woes." *Chicago Tribune*, November 11, 1990.

Meier, Barry. "Environmental Doubts on 'Green' Ads." *The New York Times*, August 11, 1990.

Moyers, Bill. "The Public Mind." (Transcript) Public Affairs Television, aired November 22, 1989.

Needham, Nancy R. "Big Bucks in Little Hands." *NEA Today*, November 1986, 16–17.

Nussbaum, Debra. "Diamond Firms Eye Teen Lode." *Adweek*, May 28, 1990, 26.

O'Connor, Helen. "Selling 'Green' to Kids Isn't Easy." *Adweek*, July 23, 1990, 17.

Ohlbaum, Edward. "A Lot of Things Still Peeve Ralph Nader." *Philadelphia Inquirer*, April 5, 1990.

Pomice, Eva. "Madison Avenue's Blind Spot." *U.S. News & World Report*, October 3, 1988, 49.

Potts, Mark. "Oil Firms Pour on 'Earth First' Message." *Washington Post*, November 14, 1990.

Randolph, Eleanor. "The No-News Generation." *The Washington Post*, June 28, 1990.

"Revolt of the Junk Receivers." *The Economist*, September 29, 1990, 24.

Riggs, Carol R. "Selling Attitudes." *D&B Reports*, July-August 1990, 28–31.

Roberts, Roxanne. "The Selling of the Prom." *The Washington Post*, May 20, 1990.

Robey, Bryant. "Demographics." *Adweek*, August 28, 1989, 41.

Rowen, Hobart. "Nader Offers New Challenges for Auto Safety." *Washington Post*, December 30, 1990.

Schwartz, John. "Stalking the Youth Market." *Newsweek* Special Issue, Summer–Fall 1990, 34–36.

Schwartz, John, with Karen Springen and Mary Hager. "It's Not Easy Being Green." *Newsweek*, November 19, 1990, 51–52.

"Selling It." (column) *Consumer Reports*, all issues 1989–1991.

Serafin, Raymond, and Gary Levin. "Ad Industry Suffers Crushing Blow." *Advertising Age*, November 12, 1990, 1.

Shapiro, Laura. "The Zap Generation." *Newsweek*, February 26, 1990, 56–57.

Springen, Karen, and Annetta Miller. "Doing the Right Thing." *Newsweek*, January 7, 1991, 42–43.

Stone, Pat. "Is It Really Organic?" *American Health*, July-August 1990, 37–40.

Sussman, Vic. "Teaching Kids How to Choose." *U.S. News & World Report*, November 5, 1990, 75.

"The Costly Future of Kids' Presents." *USA Weekend*, December 7–9, 1990, 15.

"The Green Consumer Bandwagon." *In Business*, June 1990.

"The Green Revolution." *Advertising Age*, January 29, 1991.

"The Littlest Consumers. *U.S. News & World Report*, November 5, 1990, 73–75.

"The Shoe, the Myths, the Pump." *Zillions*, August-September 1990, 13–15.

"The Zap Awards; Worst Ads of the Year." *Zillions*, December 1990-January 1991, 5–7.

Waters, Harry F. "Watch What Kids Watch." *Newsweek*, January 8, 1990, 50–52.

Wolfson, Elissa. "Greening the Golden Arches?" *E Magazine*, November-December 1990, 16–17.

Zinn, Laura J., and Antonio N. Fins. "Home Shoppers Keep Tuning In—But Investors Are Turned Off." *Business Week*, October 22, 1990, 70–72.

INDEX